New Directions in Legal Services

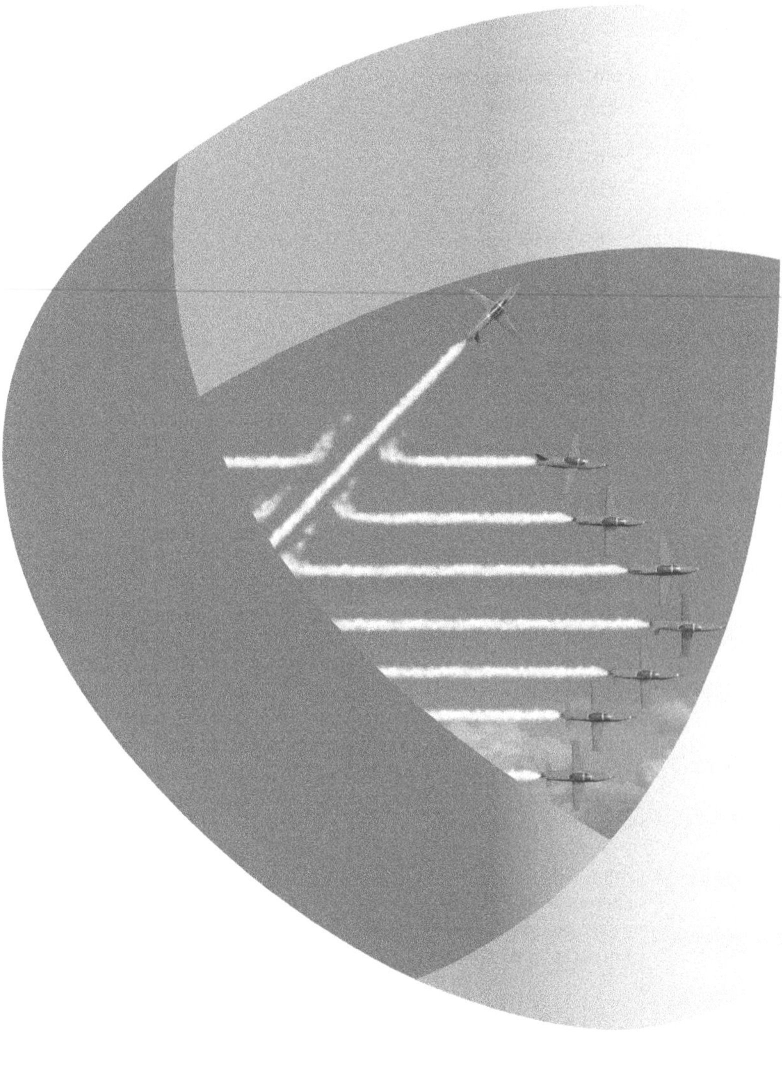

EDITED BY LAURA ARMENTANO

Commissioning editor
Laura Armentano

Editorial assistant
Edward Bowes

Published by
Globe Law and Business Ltd
3 Mylor Close
Horsell
Woking
Surrey GU21 4DD
United Kingdom
Tel: +44 20 3745 4770
www.globelawandbusiness.com

ISBN: 978-1-78358-298-3
A catalogue record for this book is available from the British Library

Contents

Executive summary

There have been a number of research papers published in recent years predicting significant further change for the legal industry. One paper found legal technology solutions could perform 30–50 per cent of the work carried out by junior lawyers today,[1] while another predicted a fall in market share among traditional firms by as much as 50 per cent within the next decade.[2] Lawyers, too, seem to agree that further change is necessary – one study found 64 per cent of lawyers think the traditional law firm business model is outdated[3] – and many are voting with their feet and taking advantage of the growing number of career routes available within the sector.

Legal services providers today need to innovate in their business models, delivery methods, and moreover in their value propositions in order to compete against competition coming in all shapes and sizes (and from unexpected quarters). They also need to work harder to attract and retain the best talent in the face of the broadening spectrum of roles and career routes that are becoming available.

New Directions in Legal Services examines the fast pace of change in the legal services sector, driven in part by new technologies, and considers what the future holds. We also look at some examples of new business models and service delivery methods that are disrupting the market, and the new approaches to pricing and profitability that are necessary to support new ways of working and delivering legal services.

The opening chapter of the book outlines the findings of research into the impact of technology on the traditional law firm business model, undertaken in 2016 by Bucerius Law School in conjunction with the Boston Consulting Group. Using the report's findings as a yardstick, Markus Hartung and Emma Ziercke of the Bucerius Center on the Legal Profession (CLP) at the Bucerius Law School, examine whether and how far legal technology has driven law firms to adjust their business models.

This is followed by a chapter from Joanna Goodman, writer, editor, and IT columnist for the *Law Society Gazette* and the Guardian Media Network – and author of *Robots in Law* – who explores five new business models that are altering the legal services landscape, driven by AI and emerging technologies.

Then, in the next chapter, Chrissie Lightfoot, CEO of Robot Lawyer LISA and CEO of EntrepreneurLawyer Limited, moves beyond current uses of cognitive computing (CC) and AI technologies in law to make some predictions about the unstoppable 'march of the machine' across the legal landscape, and she urges lawyers to prepare for a future that might be closer than you think.

In Chapter 4, John Alber, legal futurist at the ITLA, dives deep into Design Thinking and explains how this empathy-based approach to innovation can be applied to legal service design. The chapter is illustrated with successful examples from within and outside the legal sector.

Next, Debbie Epstein Henry, founder of DEH Consulting, Speaking, Writing, looks at the benefits for individual lawyers, clients, and law firms in greater acceptance of non-linear career paths in law, including: improved recruitment and retention of talent, greater ability to meet clients' expectations, and supporting and getting the most from lawyers at all stages of their careers. 'The bottom line', she says, 'is that lawyers' lives are not linear and therefore legal careers need not be either'.

Finally in this first section, Michael Roster, co-chair of the ACC Value Challenge, describes how in-house and outside counsel need to rethink the way work is priced and paid for in line with new ways of delivering legal services, and by focusing on expertise and outcomes.

The chapters in the second part of this book provide specific examples of innovative approaches to the delivery of legal services, drawn from NewLaw and traditional legal services providers, as well as in-house teams.

First, Martyn Caplan, founder and director of Lawyers Inc., describes how the 'umbrella' alternative business structure was created in response and as a solution to common concerns among lawyers, including growing pressures and demands of practice, fee earners generating more income than partners, and in particular the prevalent lack of succession (and other) planning in law firms.

This is followed by a chapter from Janvi Patel, executive chairwoman and founder of Halebury, a NewLaw business which provides flexible, scalable resourcing solutions for in-house teams, and also offers an alternative career path for in-house lawyers. She describes how the legal services model has evolved over the last 10 years, the array of new options for in-house teams, and a future collaborative, efficient, sustainable model for legal services delivery which will maximise the capabilities within the profession.

Next, Richard Tapp, company secretary and director of legal services at Carillion plc, and Fleur Kitchingman, senior vice president of legal and corporate secretary at Carillion Canada, describe the company's highly successful collaborative model for legal resourcing and explain why they believe collaboration between panel firms is vital to achieving consistency of service, quality, speed of response, and the ability to scan the horizon for future challenges.

Finally, Mike Polson, a director of Ashurst Advance and co-head of innovation for international law firm Ashurst, and Christie Guimond, R&D strategy manager for Ashurst Advance, examine how law firms can implement and sustain business model innovation. By focusing on Ashurst's integrated global service offering, Ashurst Advance, they explore how the firm was able to bring three fundamental areas of service innovation together in order to establish a clear and differentiated proposition for its clients, and they explain how Ashurst is now working to embed this model across its global business and with clients.

The message to the legal sector could not be clearer: innovate or die. As this book clearly outlines, individuals, law firms, and legal departments are accepting the challenge and are innovating alongside the NewLaw service providers that have taken root in the industry to provide a growing array of options for lawyers and clients. It truly is an exciting time to be in the business of law.

References

1. Veith, Wenzler, Hartung et al., 'How Legal Technology Will Change the Business of Law', Final Report of Bucerius Law School and The Boston Consulting Group on the impact of innovative technology on the legal sector, 2015/2016. Available at: http://www.bucerius-education.de/fileadmin/content/pdf/studies_publications/Legal_Tech_Report_2016.pdf. See also Chapter 1 of this book.
2. Beaton, G. and Kaschner, I. *Remaking Law Firms: Why & How?* ABA, 2016. See also Chapter 3 of this book.
3. Robbins, W. 'A vision of the future', *Solicitors Journal*, 4 April 2017. Available at: https://www.solicitorsjournal.com/comment/201704/vision-future.

About the authors

John Alber serves as futurist for the International Legal Technology Association. He also writes, speaks, and consults, focusing on finding practical ways to reshape the delivery of legal services to suit a future demanding excellence far beyond substantive legal skills. Prior to his current role, John led Bryan Cave LLP to become one of the most innovative firms in the world, serving as its strategic innovation partner for more than 16 years. While at Bryan Cave, he also served for seven years on the firm's operating group (its management committee). At Bryan Cave, John created one of the first practice economics consulting groups, one of the first client facing technology groups, and one of the first in-firm legal process outsourcing (LPO) organisations. The groups he created developed innovative web-based, client-centric applications that delivered legal advice to clients, managed complex workflows, and even created pleadings automatically. They also developed client-facing knowledge management, project management, project estimation, and business intelligence systems, and highly technology leveraged alternative staffing solutions for engagements of all types.

Martyn Caplan is a founder and director of Lawyers Inc. He has previously been head of commercial litigation at Fruhman Davies Livingstones and commercial litigation partner at Pannone LLP. Qualified since 1987, Martyn's experience as a practice lawyer has covered the entire spectrum of commercial litigation. He became a CEDR Accredited Mediator in 2007.

Martyn's extensive knowledge and expertise in dealing with commercial and legal partner disputes has enabled him to build a comprehensive understanding of the pitfalls and challenges of the legal profession. He is a passionate advocate of the view that to avoid vulnerability, lawyers must dedicate time and attention to the succession of their practice and their exit strategy.

Recognising that to succeed a legal practice must be built as 'a business that practices law', inspired Martyn and his business partner David Tucker to create the new legal model of Lawyers Inc.

Joanna Goodman is a freelance journalist, writer, and author. She covers business and technology topics for national publications and blue-chip corporates. She is the IT columnist for the *Law Society Gazette* and writes regular features for the *Guardian* about cutting-edge technology, brands, and media. Her favourite topics include artificial intelligence, robots and chatbots, virtual assistants, connected devices, driverless cars, and virtual and augmented reality – and she's always interested in finding out about technology that's new and different. Her professional life reflects her interests in technology, books, art, and design.

Joanna has written several short films and an independent feature film, *Alfheim's Edge* (2016). She has an MBA in strategic management from Kingston University. Joanna is based in London. She likes films, going to dance classes, and travelling to new destinations.

Christie Guimond is part of Ashurst Advance, an integrated global team within leading international law firm Ashurst, which focuses on innovation and efficiency in the delivery of legal services. Ashurst Advance combines the three fundamental areas of legal service innovation – resources, process, and technology – and works alongside Ashurst legal teams globally to respond to changing client needs in the way legal services are delivered, as well as directly supporting a number of in-house legal teams to meet their own 'more for less' challenges.

Christie is qualified as a project manager with the Association for Project Management Professionals and her experience in the legal industry over the last decade has included roles in legal project management, strategic business change, and R&D. In her current role as R&D manager for Ashurst Advance, Christie is responsible for capturing, evaluating, and deploying a wide range of innovation and change initiatives.

Markus Hartung is a lawyer and mediator. He is director of the Bucerius Center on the Legal Profession (CLP) at Bucerius Law School, Hamburg. His expertise in the framework of the CLP lies in market development and trends, management, and strategic leadership, as well as corporate governance of law firms and business models of law firms with regard to digitisation of the legal market. He is chair of the Committee on Professional Regulation of the German Bar Association (DAV).

As a lawyer he focuses on conflict management, regulatory issues, and professional indemnity issues. In addition, he advises law firms in strategy and management questions and coaches partners in management functions.

He is a regular lecturer and conference-speaker on leadership, management topics, and professional ethics, and he has written numerous articles and book chapters on these topics. He is a co-editor and author of *Wegerich/Hartung: Der Rechtsmarkt in Deutschland* ('The Legal Market in Germany') which came to the market in early 2014 and has developed into a standard reference for the German legal market. He is also co-author of 'How Legal Technology Will Change the Business of Law', a joint study of The Boston Consulting Group and the Bucerius Law School.

Debbie Epstein Henry is the founder of DEH Consulting, Speaking, Writing, and is an internationally recognised expert, consultant, best-selling author, and public speaker on careers, workplaces, women, and the law. She is also co-founder and managing director of Bliss Lawyers, a secondment firm employing high-calibre lawyers to work on temporary engagements for in-house and law firm clients. For more information, please visit www.debbieepsteinhenry.com and www.blisslawyers.com.

Fleur Kitchingman is the senior vice president of legal and corporate secretary for Carillion Canada. She is responsible for all the legal affairs of Carillion Canada and supports the business there in a diverse range of sectors and jurisdictions spanning all of Canada's provinces and territories. She is a solicitor admitted in England and Wales in 2000, and following an early career in private practice, she has held a number of senior legal positions within Carillion plc, including roles in the UK, in Carillion's Middle East operations, and more recently in Carillion Canada in her current role, since August 2014.

Fleur's interests include the management of legal practice in-house, and the implementation of legal technology and innovation to operations to improve the effectiveness and efficiency of legal services. Fleur is no stranger to the benefits of collaboration and some examples of this include leading a project which saved around £2 million by working with the Carillion legal network in the UK to develop a process for the smart procurement of external legal services on BSF projects, and collaboration with both the UK and Middle Eastern Carillion internal legal teams and CAS to devise a system for the support of transactional legal work in the Middle East from the UK.

Chrissie Lightfoot is one of the world's top female futurists. She is a prominent international legal figure, an entrepreneur, a legal futurist, legaltech investor, writer, international keynote speaker, legal and business commentator (quoted periodically in *The Times*, the *Financial Times*, and CNN), solicitor (non-practising), honorary visiting fellow at the University of Westminster School of Law, and author of best-seller *The Naked Lawyer* and *Tomorrow's Naked Lawyer*. She is CEO and founder of EntrepreneurLawyer Ltd and, as the visionary and creator of Robot Lawyer LISA (the world's first impartial AI lawyer), is CEO and co-founder of AI Tech Support Ltd (trading as Robot Lawyer LISA). In 2013 she was honoured as 'Legal Professional of the Year 2013' and a 'Top 100 International Executive'.

In 2015 LinkedIn announced Chrissie is the No.1 best-connected and most engaged woman in the legal sector (4th across all sectors). In 2017 EntrepreneurLawyer was selected by Feedspot as one of the Top 50 Entrepreneur Blogs on the web, she became an advisor to the board of the *Telegraph*'s Digital Enterprise Network, was listed as one of the Top 10 Lawyers turned Entrepreneurs in *Entrepreneur* magazine, and made the shortlist as a finalist in the Enterprise Awards. Chrissie is also an Entrepreneur Mentor at Law Without Walls; featured in *Time Magazine*, the *Financial Times*, and *Forbes*.

Janvi Patel is a NewLaw pioneer and has been spearheading operational, structural, and cultural change within the legal services industry since starting Halebury in 2007. Her aim: to create an entirely original business model to service the needs of clients and lawyers at the senior end of the market. The firm now has partnerships with clients such as BT, Sky, and Virgin Media, a growing roster of clients in the TMT and FS sectors, a team of more than 30 senior in-house lawyers who provide flexible resourcing solutions as well as strategic in-house management support to FTSE 250 and SME businesses.

Mike Polson is part of Ashurst Advance, an integrated global team within leading international law firm Ashurst, which focuses on innovation and efficiency in the delivery of legal services. Ashurst Advance combines the three fundamental areas of legal service innovation – resources, process, and technology – and works alongside Ashurst legal teams globally to respond to changing client needs in the way legal services are delivered, as well as directly supporting a number of in-house legal teams to meet their own 'more for less' challenges.

Mike is a director of Ashurst Advance and co-head of innovation for Ashurst. After a successful career as a corporate lawyer, Mike joined Ashurst to help establish and then lead its legal sourcing and business support office in Glasgow, which has grown to over 250 people in less than four years.

Michael Roster is co-chair of the Association of Corporate Counsel's Value Challenge Steering Committee. He was formerly managing partner of Morrison & Foerster's Los Angeles office as well as co-chair of the firm's Financial Services Practice Group worldwide, resident in both Los Angeles and Washington, DC.

Mike subsequently was general counsel of Stanford University, Stanford Medical Center, and Stanford Management Company – and then executive vice president and general counsel of Golden West Financial Corporation. He has also served as an outside director and vice chair of Silicon Valley Bank, chair of the Stanford Alumni Association, chair of the Association of Corporate Counsel, and chair of two start-up companies (Insert Therapeutics and Encirq). He is a former director of the California Bankers Association and the Federal Home Loan Bank of San Francisco.

Mike is currently an adjunct faculty member at USC Gould School of Law where he teaches advanced contracts. He also is a director of MDRC, a non-profit corporation based in New York that evaluates the effectiveness of government and other non-profit programs, and several years ago he chaired a project funded by two foundations that developed a private sector approach to eliminate abuses in consumer credit cards in the US.

Richard Tapp is company secretary and director of legal services for Carillion plc. He leads on legal and regulatory matters for Carillion globally, and is responsible for Carillion Advice Services, which provides a range of managed legal services offerings and resources, Richard is a solicitor, and a fellow of the Institute of Chartered Secretaries and Administrators. He holds first and post-graduate degrees in Law, together with that of Master of Business Administration.

He has led a range of innovative legal sourcing arrangements for Carillion. He is co-author of *Managing External Legal Resources* (ICSA) and *The In-House Lawyer's Toolkit* (Law Society Publishing). He is also general editor and author of a number of contributions to *The Future of the In-House Lawyer* (Law Society Publishing, 2016). He won the Most Innovative European In-House lawyer in the 2013 *FT* Innovative Lawyers awards.

Before joining Carillion, he was for six years company secretary and group legal adviser for Blue Circle Industries PLC, a FTSE 100 global heavy building materials business. He has established, run, and integrated in-house legal teams in North and South America, Europe, Australasia, the Middle East, and Asia.

Emma Ziercke is a research assistant for the Bucerius Center on the Legal Profession and a non-practising solicitor. Between 2002 and 2009, Emma worked as a corporate solicitor (managing associate) for Linklaters in London, mainly in the fields of private international M&A and public takeovers by scheme of arrangement.

Emma Ziercke studied English Law, French Law, and French Language at the University of East Anglia in Norwich and at the University of Lyon, Jean Moulin III, in France. In 2014 she completed an Executive MBA with distinction and received an award for best overall performance from Nottingham University Business School.

During her MBA studies she focused on Law Firm Management and won an award for her dissertation on gender diversity in law firms. Following her MBA studies Emma Ziercke worked as an independent adviser in the field of gender diversity. Her work as a research assistant at the Bucerius Center on the Legal Profession focuses on law firm management, gender diversity, and organisational behaviour.

Chapter 1:

Why the developments to the competence divide (and not the digital divide) will make or break the law firm business model

By Emma Ziercke, research assistant, and Markus Hartung, director, at the Bucerius Center on the Legal Profession (CLP) at the Bucerius Law School

In 2016, the Bucerius Law School in conjunction with the Boston Consulting Group, revealed in their report 'How Legal Technology will Change the Business of Law'[1] (the '2016 Report') that legal technology solutions could perform as much as 30–50 per cent of the work currently carried out by junior lawyers; firms would need to redefine key elements of their business model in order to succeed in the new world of legal technology. One year on, we examine whether legal technology has caused law firms to re-write their business models. It is evident that firms are already striving to differentiate their service offering by availing themselves of legal technology, and are benefiting from technology in enhancing their internal processes.

Other aspects of the law firm paradigm, such as revenue models and organisational structure, are reactionary and the signs of change are difficult to establish. Is legal technology driving these adjustments to the model, or are there more subtle forces at work? Some argue that the digital divide between lawyers and their clients is widening[2] as lawyers gain access to state of the art legal technology, but what about the competence divide? The traditional law firm business model was founded on an information asymmetry, and ultimately an imbalance in expertise, between the lawyer and the client which made defining the customer value proposition relatively straightforward. What will happen as information finds its equilibrium and the competence divide shrinks? To answer this question, we have to go back to basics and ask ourselves what the key attributes of the law firm business model are.

From information asymmetry to the closing competence divide: An elusive aspect of the law firm paradigm

Firms compete on the strength of their business models, but what is the law firm business model? Experts such as Clayton Christensen[3] will stipulate that a business model consists of four key elements:

1. A customer value proposition that fulfils an important job for the client in a better way than competitors' offerings;
2. A profit formula that describes how the organisation makes money delivering the value proposition;
3. The key resources; and
4. The key processes needed to deliver the value proposition.

Although this definition may be the perfect tool with which to analyse the effects of legal technology on a business model, when it comes to law firms, the first key element remains critically elusive: the customer value proposition.

One aspect of the customer value proposition that is most often overlooked is the *asymmetry* on which the very business model is founded. In the same way as doctors are revered for their medical expertise, so lawyers are sought after for their legal expertise. 'Scientia potentia ist' ('knowledge is power') and the power resides firmly with the lawyer. The asymmetry in information and expertise permeates the entire business model from the customer value proposition through to the way firms make profit and organise their resources. This divide has begun to shrink, however, not only through the increase in the number of proverbial 'Google' lawyers, but also through the changing market structure which makes information more readily available and moves expertise in-house. What will happen to the model as the asymmetry is redressed and the divide closes?

Legal expertise

Historically, businesses went to law firms because the lawyer had a greater depth of knowledge than the in-house legal team. Nowadays, corporate legal departments are reinforcing their numbers[4] and, more likely than not, filling them with ex-private practice lawyers. Hence legal expertise and knowledge has moved in-house, and the asymmetry between the lawyer and the client is 'righted'. In the English legal profession, as well as in Germany, the private practice lawyer is likely to be working with an in-house lawyer who was once a highly respected and skilled colleague and who has moved in-house, for one reason or another. Furthermore, the amount of legal information available from resources other than law firms is growing (see for example the services offered by Thomson Reuters). Thus, the value proposition of 'fulfilling an important job' for a client becomes a challenge when the client has at least as much expertise as the lawyer, and the same access to information.

Leverage

The asymmetry does not stop there. Law firms' profit formulae reside in achieving a sufficiently high leverage (the average ratio of associates per equity partner). A higher leverage translates into higher equity-partner incomes, and thus higher PEP (profit per equity partner). When used as a financial, rather than organisational tool, leverage disregards the quintessence of the customer value proposition. A high leverage (as well as an unrealistically low leverage) is not in the client's best interests. While a competence asymmetry was the cornerstone of the business paradigm, clients (begrudgingly or otherwise) simply paid their bills. Without the requisite information, the client could not assess whether the matter should be staffed with two associates per partner or five associates per partner. As long as the work was done on time and to budget, the client cared little for 'how' the firm organised its resources to provide the service. Now clients are acutely aware of 'over-lawyering' and will challenge law firms' decisions on how to staff transactions, and even decisions on which seniority of lawyer carries out which tasks.

Opacity

Finally, the overall lack of transparency in how law firms organise their resources in order to provide the client with the service previously allowed firms to charge the client based on a simple billable hour formula at the end of the process. Brief narratives describing the work carried out were provided to clients, mostly on request. Thus the information asymmetry was, once again, weighted in the law firm's favour. With the advent of highly advanced billing systems, clients can now see in real time how much the transaction is costing. Accordingly, the balance of information power has shifted to the client.

How legal technology will change the business of law

A brief recap: The 2016 Report ('How Legal Technology will Change the Business of Law') created a snapshot of both big and small law firms' current business models and identified the new imperatives which will lead to change in the future, namely:

1. Stronger competition from boutique firms in respect of bespoke work, and from legal-process outsourcing providers and legal-tech vendors in respect of standardised work; and
2. Evolving client expectations, which are becoming more sharply focused on efficiency (quicker, more tailored advice), along with a call for greater transparency on fees and more seamless collaboration between internal and external lawyers.

What does this mean for the business model? Beginning with the heart of any business model, the *value proposition*, the job the client wants fulfilled is no longer restricted to pure legal advice. The report revealed that firms will need to offer *additional* services such as legal project management (i.e. professionally led project management), case management tools, legal analytics and decision-support solutions, as well as acting as an outsourcing manager for legal services. Some firms could even become 'legal tech vendors' selling legal technology to their clients or advising clients on purchasing legal technology, and/or finding the appropriate legal outsourcing partner for standardised work.

As the value proposition changes, so must the *revenue model*. The report points out that the billable hour impedes the adoption of new value propositions. A solution would be to adopt partial fixed pricing based on quantifiable success against clearly defined deliverables, as is already common in other professional service industries.

How will the *operating model* change? The report suggested that firms will need to outsource low-skilled legal work and automate high-volume but standardised tasks. Work will be differentiated internally between complex non-standard tasks, and those where legal-tech and legal process outsourcing can be used to advantage. Firms' cost structures will also change significantly as technology becomes a larger element of its base cost along with employee wages.

Finally, the report emphasised that the *organisational model* will need to change in two key ways: firstly there will be a much lower ratio of junior lawyers to partners; secondly there will be different, adjacent roles of project manager and tech manager. The end result is the metamorphosis of the pyramid into a rocket shaped organisation, thus leading to the conclusion that the use of technology will reduce the ratio of junior lawyers to partners by up to three-quarters.

Is legal technology really changing the law firm model?

What has changed since 2016? Are firms already re-inventing their business models? Where are they making the most progress? Taking the traditional business model analysis together with our interpretation of the information and competence asymmetry aspect, we can gain an extraordinary insight into the way business models are evolving.

The value proposition: Complexity and bespoke information

Firms are making the most adjustments with regard to their *value proposition*. Legal technology has offered firms a new tool box with which to design their service offerings. Firms from high-street practices to Magic Circle firms have already begun to provide clients with additional services *outside of* the traditional sphere of legal advice.

Legal project management

Legal project management (LPM) is the primary area in which firms are able to deliver the most value. The legal project management of huge, complex, and international matters, such as class actions (for example, Volkswagen) or M&A (for example, AB InBev/SABMiller) is not only a question of sheer 'manpower', but increasingly of high quality, professional project management – resources and expertise which clients are unlikely to have in-house. Thus, even if the information or competence asymmetry is redressed, a *process* asymmetry remains. A transaction that requires regulatory hurdles to be met in over 20 different countries, or tens of thousands of different contracts in different languages to be reviewed, is beyond the logistical capabilities of most in-house teams.

This need can be met in various ways. The firm and its lawyers can simply demonstrate a superior legal process management capability when dealing with complex and multi-dimensional matters, usually by training their lawyers in legal project management (see for example, Allen & Overy or Herbert Smith Freehills). Other aspects of legal project management include offering better ways to collaborate, such as the *Deal Room* (Dentons) or *dealVault* (Norton Rose Fulbright), both of which facilitate document review and sharing between internal and external lawyers. Alternatively, some firms are offering clients integrated tools for project managing, such as Baker & McKenzie's *iG360* for information governance. Clients can access the tool at any time, online or via an app, and even manage costs through the tool. In addition, firms are providing legal outsourcing managed services such as Berwin Leighton Paisner's *Lawyers on Demand*, Pinsent Masons' *Vario* or Eversheds' *Agile*.

Legal data analytics

Firms are enhancing the value proposition by making *legal data analytics* available to clients. Examples are: DLA's *Cyber Trak* (with Blue Edge Lab) which provides online access to information on cyber security worldwide, but in particular, maps certain standards onto the client organisation's compliance framework to identify areas of compliance and potential concern; and Allen & Overy's *Margin Matrix* (in conjunction with Deloitte), a derivatives compliance system designed to help banks deal with new regulatory requirements. The system codifies the law in various jurisdictions and systematises the drafting based on an automated legal analysis. Such services can overlap with legal project management services, to the extent they replace the need to appoint and manage separate providers across the world. Other examples include Linklaters' *Verifi*, and DWF's counter-fraud service, which analyses for example, fraudulent insurance claims to predict claimants' behaviour and help clients develop strategies to counter such fraud.

Access to information

While legal tech opens a completely new access to justice (A2J) in the business to customer (B2C) area, things are different in business to business (B2B). The righting of the information asymmetry opens up additional ways for firms to grasp the value proposition. Although the client and the lawyer may be on a par with their legal expertise and access to information, we live in a time of information overload with the result that finding a path through the plethora of information is a valuable proposition. Take for example the general counsel of a global company, the sheer magnitude of information that GC would be required to know about overseas regulations and laws makes it impossible to manage. This is where firms are stepping in, and providing their clients with information in a succinct, user-friendly, and tailored way.

The information is presented in different forms; a newsletter, on a website, as a video (see for example CM Murray's Resource Library), through a secure portal, for free, or as part of a subscription. The amount of information can be varied, from simple guides to detailed reports. The service can be merely to keep clients up to date with developments in the law (see for example Hogan Lovells' Brexit Taskforce), or can pull together regulations from all over the world. A prime example of the latter is Baker & McKenzie's Global Merger Analysis Platform, in which merger control rules in 120 different jurisdictions are summarised, together with real-time updates and a report-generating function.

Equally, DLA Piper's Global Patent Tool which summarises patent law and dispute resolution procedures in over 100 jurisdictions, at different levels of detail from country guides to full handbooks, also demonstrates how the righting of the information asymmetry has resulted in firms making the provision of complex information in a user-friendly form part of their service offering.

Law firms as legal tech consultants?

There is little evidence that firms are moving directly into the *legal technology consultancy* arena. Eversheds Sutherland LLP's consulting arm (ES Legal Consulting) has, jointly with Repstor, developed a matter and contract management application, which it markets to in-house legal teams. Otherwise, firms are slowly building up their reputation as users of, and eventually experts in, legal technology. Berwin Leighton Paisner's Talk Tech, is a prime example of this approach. The online portal is run by Berwin Leighton Paisner and brings together general counsels who are interested in legal technology and offers them a platform for discussing experiences, opportunities, and challenges in leveraging legal tech. Finally, some firms are offering adjacent services, such as providing legal training to clients (see for example DLA Piper's Future Legal Leaders).

Revenue model: Client or lawyer managed?

There is less evidence that firms are actually changing their revenue models. Naturally, there is the ostensible trend that more clients are seeking alternative fee arrangements. In the UK for example, GlaxoSmithKline announced last year that over 80 per cent of its law firm fees were now on an alternative fee arrangement basis. Law firms continue, however, to use leverage as an on/off switch for profit, and in a period of financial uncertainty, the trend is towards low leverage. Again, the key issue with the law firm revenue model resides in the shifting information asymmetry; clients increasingly have real time access to 'the clock', and can see at any time how many hours have been worked and what fees have been incurred, leaving the firm nowhere to hide when it comes to inefficient work, poor delegation, or overly high leverage ratios. Client-lawyer collaboration may be increasing, but it is also changing the way lawyers work, and can lead to a swing from lawyers' 'command and control' approach to clients' 'micro-managing'. The 2016 Report noted that firms need to re-consider the billable hour. Despite the dramatic shift in information equilibrium, firms will struggle to make sudden changes to the billable hour regime. The billable hour has entwined itself in the very fabric of law firm organisation: performance and remuneration criteria, work allocation decisions, promotion criteria, work methodology, appetite for non-client related work (such as know-how, innovation, team management, mentoring, and leadership), organisational structure, working culture, and even lawyers' appreciation of their own self-worth are rooted in the billable hour as the token measuring unit.

Organisation of resources: Early signs?

A law firm's primary resource is its lawyers, and increasingly, its technology base. The 2016 Report predicted that law firm structures will move from a pyramid to a rocket, as more experts are retained and the new roles of legal project manager and technology manager are introduced. It seems to us that the predicted changes have not yet taken place, even not yet begun; at the time of writing, the latest statistics for the profession are not yet fully published, but there are some interesting initial indicators. In the UK, the Spring 2017 trainee retention rates for top City firms were only marginally down on those from 2016 (see reports in, for example, *The Lawyer*), with most firms still being around the 80 per cent mark. Deloitte reported in their quarterly Legal Sector Survey Update that firm headcounts were up around 1–2 per cent, whereas the *Legal Week*'s analysis (in conjunction with Smith & Williamson) of firms' 2015–2016 financial accounts revealed a previous 3.6 per cent increase in headcount. Although the analysis did not differentiate between lawyers and potentially 'new' roles, spending on salaries increased last year by 4.8 per cent. It may be too early to tell, but firms do not appear to be in a hurry to convert their pyramid to a rocket.

Key processes: Opacity

The 2016 Report noted that firms may move from handling all tasks in-house to out-sourcing low-skilled work. This is borne out to the extent that top city firms in the UK (such as Allen & Overy and Herbert Smith Freehills) have 'low-cost centres' outside of their London hubs. Others are using data analytics to allocate workflow more efficiently (see for example Ashursts' 'blind' work allocation system), although this is still in its infancy. An increasing number of firms are investing in software programs and artificial intelligence (such as KIRA and RAVN) to provide answers to standardised questions. Some firms are actually collaborating with clients to produce a tool for standardising routine work for the client's benefit (see for example a simple collaboration between Pinsent Masons and Everton Football Club to create a contract generator for player transfers).

Information equilibrium, but in a dynamic market?

There is evidence that, one year on, firms are already altering their business models supported by legal technology to deal with the shifting asymmetries in information and expertise. Firms are focused on changing the value proposition and are taking advantage of the new toolkit provided by legal technology to do so. Spurred on by the fact that the client knows as much, if not more than the lawyer, firms are focusing on offering legal project management, legal analytics, and bespoke information. The key processes needed to provide the new value proposition are also developing significantly and even being used as a new value proposition in their own right. Changes to the revenue model are more sluggish, despite the fact that the information asymmetry has been corrected and the client has almost become the cost manager. The organisation of resources, like the revenue model, is embedded in law firm organisational behaviour and culture, and firms are therefore slow to adapt.

Is the emerging model robust enough? All things being equal, the new value proposition can be replicated by other firms, indeed by other players. The crux of the problem is that business models are dynamic and depend upon who else is offering the same or similar services. Our analysis is thus only a snapshot, as the success or failure of a business model depends on how it interacts with the models of other players in the industry (on which one would need to dedicate a separate chapter). The competitive advantage obtained by differentiating the legal service offering is only short-lived. What will be the new value proposition? An improved delivery method? An additional service offering? Perhaps a radically different value proposition – the game-changing opportunity to solve a problem for the client that has never been solved before? One thing is clear, firms will need to adapt the operational aspects of their business models much more quickly in order to keep up with the need to constantly offer new and differentiated value propositions, as the competence divide is closed and information continues to find its equilibrium.

References

1. Veith, Wenzler, Hartung et al., 'How Legal Technology Will Change the Business of Law', Final Report of Bucerius Law School and The Boston Consulting Group

on the impact of innovative technology on the legal sector, 2015/2016. Available at: http://www.bucerius-education.de/fileadmin/content/pdf/studies_publications/Legal_Tech_Report_2016.pdf.

2. See for example the Eversheds/Sutherland/Winmark 2016 Looking Glass Report.
3. Clayton Christensen, Professor of Business Administration, Harvard Business School and author of numerous articles and books on innovation and business model innovation. See www.claytonchristensen.com.
4. In fact, early indicators from the Law Society of England and Wales Annual Statistics Report 2016 are that the number of solicitors working in-house has risen to 22 per cent of all practising certificate holders.

Chapter 2:
AI and five new business models for legal services

By Joanna Goodman, writer, editor, and IT columnist for the Law Society Gazette *and the Guardian Media Network. Author of* Robots in Law.

Although artificial intelligence (AI) has been heralded as the latest game-changer in legal services, it is a natural part of the legal IT revolution that started with market liberalisation and tech commoditisation which produced Alternative Business Structures (ABSs), Alternative Fee Arrangements (AFAs), and workflow automation software for fixed-price volume/standardised legal work. Another catalyst for AI in the legal sector, like other sectors, is the general take-up of cloud computing which levelled the legal IT playing field and is the basis for big data analysis – and any data analysis – as it does not require infinite data storage capabilities. While these advances have driven AI software development and adoption, AI itself has changed the direction of legal technology, as an innovation enabler – leading to the creation of new business models for the legal services industry. This chapter looks at some examples of these.

My definition of legal AI

The starting point has to be a definition of AI in relation to legal services. AI takes software beyond straightforward functionality because it can also do some of the things that humans can do with their brains.

While AI in other sectors covers complex technical processes, motion, sound or vision, and behavioural and sentiment analysis involving, for example, consumer preferences or patient responses, and uses the output to develop new products, services, and solutions, most legal AI software deals with data analysis, extraction, and comparison to deliver legal processes and support (strategic/legal) decision-making. It incorporates cognitive computing, which combines natural language processing (NLP) and machine learning (ML), which enable it to 'understand' instructions and carry out some of the tasks that lawyers do.

In a recent presentation, I created this equation to explain how legal AI software works:

Structured/unstructured data + NLP + ML
= intelligent processes/relevant responses

This is not necessarily straightforward as the initial/underlying data can be in different formats, under different ownership, and reside in different repositories – i.e. it can be documents, audio, video, email etc, and it can belong to the firm, its lawyers, clients, or other stakeholders, or it can be external data that is available publicly or via a subscription and used to inform/support a legal matter.

Four main legal AI applications

The following examples of legal AI demonstrate some of its applications to mergers and acquisitions (M&A); legal research; compliance; and prediction. These are not exclusive, but they are the starting points for legal AI hitting the mainstream.

M&A

Legal AI software such as RAVN iManage or Luminance is used to extract information from internal or external data. The software 'reads' multiple documents contemporaneously and extracts the relevant information. Both of these tools are a direct development from the sophisticated search engines used for technology assisted review (TAR) at the e-discovery (or e-disclosure) stage of litigation, whereby large volumes of documents are analysed for relevance using sampling to train the software. RAVN iManage and Luminance take this further because the AI engine 'reads' all the documents instead of just a sample, and it reads them at the same time and in the same way, whereas the human element of sampling will necessarily include some differences in approach and understanding.

The differentiator is horizontal scalability – the ability to replicate tasks multiple times simultaneously enables AI software to be configured to handle work that while it may be routine, is not repetitive. For example, RAVN Systems' original legal application was Berwin Leighton Paisner's legal 'robot' LONald, which was developed to undertake due diligence for real estate transactions by connecting with the Land Registry website to verify property details. RAVN iManage has since been applied to multiple tasks. Last year it hit the headlines for its role in the Serious Fraud Office's investigation into corruption at Rolls-Royce, where an algorithm was trained to process 600,000 documents a day. This produced a massive saving of time and money as manual document processing was only covering 3,000 documents a day!

Luminance, a pay-as-you-go online AI engine, is closer to the TAR process as it requires no training – you simply upload the entire document set and the software identifies correlations and anomalies. Put simply, it reads and auto-classifies large volume document sets. Luminance 'reads' like a human, not like a search engine. For example, it analyses information in different formats – including images – and it will identify observational anomalies such as a document that is missing pages, as well as textual ones.

Kira Systems was developed by former lawyer Noah Waisberg and his team as a tool for reviewing contracts during the due diligence process. Like RAVN iManage and Luminance, it is about extracting and comparing information, but it sits at the opposite end of the legal AI spectrum from Luminance, in that the software is licensed to the firm, which trains it on its own data. Kira Systems is only involved in the initial set up, which includes configuring the system and teaching people in the firm to train it and work with it.

The ability to set the data points for analysis, and point the system at particular data enables each firm to develop its own, bespoke AI tools, which may or may not relate to due diligence. Kira Systems has enabled several firms to create client facing tools that add value to the business, in addition to internal efficiencies. For example, Clifford Chance uses Kira to create white-label Clifford Chance contracts for its clients to use; Freshfields has trained Kira to work on German real estate contracts, and Kemp Little has built a Brexit tool to enable its clients to check contracts against legislative changes resulting from the Brexit process. Kira is used by alternative legal service providers Axiom and Elevate to support corporate legal departments.

Turning to corporate legal AI, Berlin-based Leverton, which is used predominantly by legal departments in the real estate industry, applies deep learning (a branch of machine learning that trains algorithms to recognise patterns in digital data, including text, audio, and images), to extract provisions from legal documents in the form of attributes – what a clause means rather than what it states. Clients upload documentation to the Leverton platform, abstract it, and validate it – some data may require validation by multiple parties – to create a report.

Leverton's 'attributes' make provisions language agnostic and its ability to create summaries means lawyers no longer need to create abstracts of new precedents, legislation, or regulations. The core attributes of a contract written in German can be understood by a Spanish or Chinese party to a transaction, or replicated to become part of a new contract in French or Italian without translation or interpretation. This also enables corporate legal departments to share knowledge and expertise with international offices and clients.

Legal research

The best-known AI-powered legal research engine is ROSS Intelligence which was branded the first 'robot lawyer'. ROSS is a virtual knowledge worker which specialises in bankruptcy-related legal research. It combines NLP with IBM Watson's cognitive engine and was first employed by the bankruptcy practice at US law firm BakerHostetler, supporting attorneys by finding appropriate precedents and other documents. Attorneys type in their questions in natural language and ROSS searches through legal precedents to produce evidence-based answers, basically replacing some of the work traditionally undertaken by professional support lawyers (PSLs).

Compliance

Neota Logic is an expert system that creates code-free apps for applying legislation and regulation to legal queries, combining legal knowledge, reasoning, and judgement to provide self-service real-time legal advice. It has been used to create specific compliance apps, for example, Littler Mendleson's ComplianceHR, and provides a platform for Taylor Wessing among others to develop interactive apps that clients can use to find out in real-time whether they are subject to particular rules and regulations. Like Kemp Little's Brexit tool, built on the Kira Systems platform, this is another example of AI's horizontal scalability: (relevant, but not necessarily identical) initial legal advice can be delivered concurrently to an unlimited number of parties.

Prediction

Legal AI is increasingly focusing on online justice – partly because of its ability and potential to save (public services, lawyers, and parties to litigation) time and money. Commercially, there has been a growing movement towards helping clients and law firms predict the case outcomes with sufficient accuracy to guide decision-making. Two examples of this are LexisNexis Lex Machina and Premonition, which use big data analysis and algorithms to provide evidence-based forecasts.

Two legal AI differentiators

As these examples demonstrate, legal AI offerings share two main qualities that differentiate it from traditional, legacy, and mainstream legal IT:

1. Legal AI is narrow – each application does a specific task or set of tasks. Leading vendors fall into two categories: off-the-shelf products that include AI; and AI software that can be trained and adapted to a law firm's specific work.
2. Legal AI is new – so there are no long-established brands or legacy technology. AI's vast potential, its propensity to attract media interest, and its untapped potential means it is attracting a new generation of technologists, and helping to shape a new generation of legal technology, legal services, and lawyers.

Five new business models

New business model 1: The lawtech start-up

AI is certainly helping legal services move away from the establishment – rather than traditional law firms, lawtech start-ups are changing the legal services brand. As legal AI is relatively new – it first hit the press in 2014-2015, it has helped to galvanise the legal start-up dynamic which continues to see plenty of new offerings, many of which involve facilitating access to legal advice and legal services; helping law firms and their clients create smart documents; improving processes such as document analysis, clause extraction, and spotting similarities and anomalies. Another focus area involves helping law firms develop business, connecting businesses and individuals with legal advisers (law firms and barristers) and matching lawyers to business opportunities.

Legal AI and other emerging technology is shifting the relationship between legal service providers and their customers: intelligent, automated decision-making is becoming the first step in resolving certain issues, meaning that in many cases the first contact a customer has with the provider is via technology. This is likely to change further with the growth of blockchain-enabled smart contracts. This change in the first contact point is perhaps the biggest technology-driven change to the legal business model, so far.

The start-up dynamic is also affecting the law firm procurement model. Law firm decision-makers are struggling with a tidal wave of relatively similar new offerings. Firms now have a massive choice of different smart contracts and document analysis engines. Another consideration for mid-market firms with a limited IT budget is the risk of relying on online tools and technology (nearly all AI software is cloud-based due to the processing power it requires) from a start-up which may not be around in a few years' time (most start-ups fail or are acquired). Therefore they stick with major vendors, who are developing and acquiring AI applications. The iManage/RAVN acquisition is a case in point, as it gives iManage customers a risk-free opportunity to apply RAVN's AI software.

However, this low-risk option is not a market differentiator, so firms are looking to boost their brand by adding on 'innovation' in the form of a start-up incubator, or wholly owned subsidiary, or at the very least an innovation department or 'space'. In this way, AI is changing the desired brand image of legal service providers.

New business model 2: Online legal advice

Online legal services have been around for a while, with commoditised legal services using white labelled automated workflows.

AI takes the online legal app further, beyond a straightforward decision tree, with law firms using generalist and legal-specific AI platforms to create narrow applications that provide initial guidance and tailored advice on legislative changes like Brexit (see Kemp Little's tool, above) and GDPR as well as bespoke client-facing tools (like Clifford Chance's contract tool).

Furthermore, AI powered 'smart' advice does not necessarily entail significant investment in an off-the-shelf software platform. Alan Larkin, director at Family Law Partners in Brighton, has used intelligent technology to respond to government cuts in family legal services and the subsequent increase in the number of litigants in person.

Larkin explains the rationale that led him to build an online portal providing guidance on family law, including break-ups, division of assets and child maintenance payments. 'I understand the rationale behind proposals for an online court, but by the time cases reach court, the damage is already done. If local authorities developed an online portal where people could access advice, some of them could be directed to mediation and potentially avoid court altogether.'

Having obtained matched funding from Innovate UK, and employed a PhD computer science student from the University of Brighton under the knowledge transfer partnership scheme, Larkin used a free tool – WordPress Gravity Forms – to develop a triage system for family law, which includes a conditional logic questionnaire that produces automated emails that can be sent to or shared with a co-parent, lawyer, or other adviser.

These customer-facing online tools provide potential clients with a starting point, and represent a business development tool for law firms, as the next step – consulting a lawyer – is on the same website.

Other new business models actually replace a lawyer. For example, legal start-up Farewill offers an online service for wills you can create, amend, and store (but not sign, yet) online.

Common questions about online legal services include 'Is all this really AI?' 'How does AI take this beyond a straightforward questionnaire?'. The difference is that these engines are not a box-ticking exercise. They are about understanding natural language queries to ascertain what sort of question is being asked in order to direct the inquiry to the right answer, or adviser.

The rationale – in terms of extending access to legal services and saving time and money – as well as the results produced these 'smart' online tools are also the basis for the 'chatbot lawyer' business model.

New business model 3: The legal chatbot

Chatbots are 2017's big news. In the legal sector, they divide into two categories: the altruistic – and free – model designed to extend access to legal services and support access to justice, and the commercial model, designed to facilitate a legal process, either within a law firm, or as a customer facing business tool. They are usually built on general AI platforms – IBM Watson and Facebook Messenger – and narrowly designed to deliver a specific set of services.

Joshua Browder set up DoNotPay to challenge parking tickets and having successfully challenged over £3 million in parking tickets, he moved on to help combat homelessness and immigration issues. Browder has since expanded the service to deal with over 1,000 legal questions and is creating free bots for law firms and others.

Elexirr started out as LawBot, an online service created by a group of Cambridge University law students to offer free advice to victims of crime. Initially, it was positioned as a free service similar to DoNotPay, but it subsequently evolved into LawBot X which extended the system across seven jurisdictions, but was no longer wholly altruistic as it included commercial elements, including outcome estimates for predicting the success of a case and a referral service to law firms as well as a business development system for law firms and corporate analytics capability. Now rebranded as Elexirr, its founders plan to launch a crypto currency to fund further growth.

Commercial customer facing legal services include AI Tech Support's

Legal Intelligence Support Assistant (LISA), developed by legal futurist Chrissie Lightfoot. LISA, an online non-disclosure agreement generator for entrepreneurs and small businesses who may not be able to consult a lawyer. Because LISA is impartial, it is able to represent both or multiple parties to an agreement, which would present a conflict of interest for a human lawyer or law firm. Another chatbot, Billy Bot, connects lawyers/ clients with barristers and mediators.

In April 2017, business intelligence (BI) and analytics company Helm360 launched Termi, a voice-activated chatbot built on Microsoft's cognitive services platform, that interrogates Thomson Reuters Elite 3E financial management system via Skype, Microsoft Team, or a web browser. As Bim Dave, executive vice-president, products and services, explains, Termi will enable lawyers and managers to request billing and other management information using natural language. Termi is a voice-activated tool that appears on the screen as an avatar. Dave plans to build it into a proactive bot that delivers information that is tailored to each user.

Termi promises to be different because it is a voice-activated virtual assistant, more like a Siri or Amazon Alexa, for client and management information; and it expedites internal processes rather than client services. In future, law firms' business support teams could include cognitive workers similar to IPSoft's Amelia, which acts as a service desk agent at SEB bank. Although we are unlikely to see robot lawyers in the near future, the scene is set for robot PSLs and PAs!

Emerging new business model: Conversational legal commerce using voice as a platform

The winner of the online courts hackathon, held in London in July 2017 was CoLin (Courts online) – Your Legal Pathfinder, a friendly digital assistant accessed via the Amazon Echo. CoLin used a voice interface to provide user-friendly legal guidance and advice about common real-life issues using a familiar consumer platform. CoLin, produced by a team formed by The Law Society and NewLaw firm Wavelength Law which combines legal services with legal engineering – another new business model featured below. Although CoLin was a proof of concept and not a complete product, it is an indication of the direction of legal AI.

In May 2017, Thomson Reuters Elite introduced Workspace Assistant, which enables lawyers to access Elite 3E and its partner products using a voice interface via Alexa-enabled devices. This allows lawyers to enter and track billable hours and allocate them to a specific client matter, calculate time spent on individual matters, and ask Alexa questions about billable hours. As Workspace Assistant deals with financial information, consideration has been given to security and to the possibility of Alexa 'mishearing' an entry. Workplace Assistant is hosted by Elite, so the entire process operates within the firm's security walls and each entry is reviewed and approved by the user.

New business model 4: The legal platform as a service

AI is shifting the legal business model from the client side too as legal departments are changing the way they handle internal legal issues. Here AI-powered platform Riverview Law includes a triage system which organises and classifies the queries coming into a corporate legal department and immediately decides whether they can be dealt with internally or referred to external legal counsel.

Riverview Law's Kim (knowledge, information, meaning) is an AI platform powering a range of virtual assistants that together ensure that legal work is undertaken to a consistent standard and managed efficiently. Like ROSS and DoNotPay, Kim is built on the IBM Watson platform. It enables users to create code-free software applications for specific legal tasks and includes a triage process for allocating work appropriately.

Axiom, an alternative legal services provider to large corporations, recently launched AxiomAI, a programme designed to improve the efficiency of its contract work. This basically includes deploying existing platforms, for instance Kira Systems, to automate key provisions, as well as developing and testing new legal AI tools.

AxiomAI is an acknowledgement from a well-established player that because legal AI applications are narrow, implementation means addressing technology integration issues – as each AI application handles a set of specific tasks, legal AI tools need to interface smoothly with other technology and processes.

This is a key consideration for law firms, which until legal AI appeared were moving towards standardisation, perhaps influenced by the accountancy/consultancy model as the Big Four accountancy firms venture further into the legal services market.

While magic circle firms are able to bring together multiple AI and other tools and technology into a bespoke technology architecture, this is a key consideration for mid-size and other law firms with budgetary constraints.

The situation is exacerbated by the fact that legal AI differs from conventional legal software in that it is evolving too fast for firms to be able to apply a deterministic strategy – because we cannot anticipate the speed and direction of progress in the next five years, for example. Furthermore, legal IT consultants are experienced in integrating mainstream software systems and applications, but because AI is new, few if any have experience with AI integration in multiple firms. This has created a gap in the consultancy market for a new breed of vendor-independent experts: the legal engineers.

New business model 5: The legal engineer

The legal engineer is a hybrid role which includes software implementation and training (training software as well as people!), preparing data and basically filling the implementation gap between legal service providers and emerging tech. Wavelength Law was a first mover, and there are now more examples, including Hannan Hashmi, whose contract analytics platform Codify Law was winner of Made@Cityaward. 'I see myself as a legal engineer – essentially someone with a legal background who gets into coding: the marriage of law and technology,' he explained in an interview with Future Lawyer blogger Emily Albion.[1]

Only time will tell whether legal engineering is a new business model or a temporary solution that another new business model will render obsolete as legal AI becomes the 'new normal' and more legal AI offerings follow the example of Kira Systems and introduce APIs that enable AI applications to integrate with each other and with other popular legal IT systems such as HighQ.

Will AI eventually change the law firm business model?

There is much discussion, particularly at legal AI events around whether AI will irreversibly change the law firm business model. Legal AI is already changing roles by automating more tasks, and creating new roles that work with the outputs of AI software. Law firms are employing more data scientists and business analysts and perhaps they will require fewer PSLs. And, because it is automating work AI is raising questions around legal education.

Eventually, widespread take-up may change the law firm model – fewer trainees doing repetitive tasks; more data analysts, and people who train AI software on a firm's own documents and precedents. Instead of training people, perhaps L&D will be training machines.

AI is certainly changing law firm culture. Lawyers are getting accustomed to inputting data into AI applications – and working with outputs, as well as using AI powered research engines and specific applications, like Trademark Now, an AI-powered application that speeds up trademark search, analysis, and protection. And they are using AI platforms to build their own AI-powered tools and services.

But thus far legal AI is replacing discrete tasks, not roles. It is still too narrow to threaten lawyers' jobs, notwithstanding the media hype that has persisted for the best part of two years. Indications are that the legal sector has not reached maximum or optimal automation, but because law and legal services are society's framework and involves human concepts of fairness and justice, it is inevitable that there will always be a point at which human clients (and by human I include companies) will require human advice or involvement in deeply personal or high-risk corporate or commercial matters. So, it is unlikely that we will come to rely on robot lawyers. Or, indeed, robot technologists.

Reference

1. http://blog.lawbore.net/2017/08/meet-hannan-hashmi-winner-of-madecity-and-legal-engineer/.

Chapter 3: What is the next big thing for legal services?

By Chrissie Lightfoot, CEO of Robot Lawyer LISA and CEO of EntrepreneurLawyer Limited. Author of The Naked Lawyer *and* Tomorrow's Naked Lawyer.

As a futurist, an entrepreneur, and a lawyer, I always get asked, 'What do you think is the next big thing in the legal world?'

I begin my response with a catch-all reply: 'The next big thing is anything that helps you attract and keep a client. No clients equal no business. A bit of a cliché, I know. But you must constantly rethink how to do things better using the latest research, thinking, and innovations.' In 2008 I commented that the next 'big thing' would be the adoption of social media and social networking, providing an innovative, cost-effective, smart way to market, brand, and sell using the latest in digital technology.

Facebook's founder, Mark Zuckerberg, in 2010 remarked: 'There's going to be an opportunity over the next five years or so to pick any industry and rethink it.' True to form, the legal world caught on to this latest wave of 'rethinking' – but it took far longer than in other professions and industries. It has taken more than eight years for social media to be widely adopted and truly embraced in the mainstream legal ecosystem.

Fast-forward three years from 2008 to 2011, during which I would answer with my catch-all reply and add smart technologies, such as relationship intelligent products; cognitive computing (CC); artificial intelligence (AI); and robotic automation technologies.

Leap forward another three years to 2014 and, in a nutshell, I believed the next big thing for legal was adopting a variety of fee-earning and business processes that encompass AI technologies, and which blend human talent and machine intelligence, delivering all kinds, and enabling new kinds, of legal services.

Today, smart CC and AI technologies exist that are available to pervade every aspect of fee-earning and business processes within a law firm, including marketing, business development, and customer relationship management.

Suspicions and reinventions

Not surprisingly, it has been a slow burn for these pioneering smart technologies to 'break into' the legal world. It still remains a huge challenge for the vast majority, due to the same suspicions and cautious approach that lawyers and law firms hold towards anything that may promulgate change or cause major disruption – or they simply do not understand. Not unlike how social media and social networking were viewed with scepticism back in 2008, so too is emerging intelligence – augmented and artificial – at present.

However, due to the evolution of AI and its potential impact on the legal ecosystem, Professor Richard Susskind recently warned that the legal profession has five years to reinvent itself, and the Riverview Law CEO, Karl Chapman, has predicted that the use of AI will be mainstream in the legal profession by 2020. I too have long held the belief that the profession needs to reinvent itself, and in 2011 declared that the impact of AI and robots would be felt by 2016 or thereabouts, but certainly before 2020, and definitely not in decades' time as Tony Williams predicted in the Jomati Report, 'Civilisation 2030'.

I held and hold steadfast in this view, despite ridicule and scoffing, because we, the human race, constantly surprise ourselves with our technological breakthroughs. For example, when scientists were given the green light to crack the DNA code and sequence the entire human genome, everyone (scientists, futurists, thought leaders, etc.) predicted it would take 100 years; it only took eight (1995 to 2003). Fast-forward 13 years to 2016: on 10 May Harvard University hosted a closed-door conference (in absolute secrecy – no journalists allowed) with more than 100 scientists, lawyers, and business leaders to discuss the creation of a synthetic human genome and its feasibility.

The Human Genome Project (2) aims to synthesise the full human genome. This project achieved the 'green light' soon after the meeting. I have little doubt that in all likelihood it will take far less than 10 years if the previous track record and history in genome achievement is to be taken into account. Imagine the technology in the 1990s and compare it to what we have now, factor in the exponential development of technology, and what do we have?

From AlphaGo to AlphaLaw?

Drawing a parallel with exponential advancement in AI evolution and computing intelligence breakthroughs, and factoring in what could be deployed in the legal world, in March 2016 we witnessed the stunning victory of Google DeepMind's AlphaGo over Lee Se-dol, the world champion of the strategy board game Go.

DeepMind (an AI system of neural networks) was acquired by Google in 2014 and uses games as a testing ground for AI algorithms that could have real-world applications. AlphaGo was imbued with the ability to learn through the human-like process of practice and study. It is not a hand-crafted programme in which software engineers distil information from, for example, a human player's head into specific rules and heuristics. AlphaGo's founder, Demis Hassabis, comments that an aspect of 'intuition' has been introduced into the neural networks, a characteristic which distinguishes top Go players.

The same could be said about top lawyers, lawyering, and legal service provision. In a handful of years – from the introduction of chess-playing computer programme Deep Blue in 1996 to AlphaGo's self-learning in 2016 – we have reached a point where a machine proved its superiority over a world-class human being's creativity and intuitive insights.

The fact that Lee Se-dol has since beaten AlphaGo does not detract from the significant step forward made in machine-learning capabilities. After all, even Hassabis was surprised at the rate of progress he and his team achieved in such a short timeframe – 18 months, from inception to triumph.

I cannot imagine an 18-month-old baby being able to study and learn at the same rate as AlphaGo, can you? There is, therefore, a possibility, in theory at least, that a machine could learn through practice and study to become a world champion lawyer. And this is deeply significant.

But until such time as an AlphaLaw champion lawyer exists (which may be sooner than we all anticipate), let us deal with the reality in a legal world where:

- Smart CC, AI, and robot technologies in relation to the four key elements of legal service provision – commoditisation, research, reasoning, and judgement – exist and can support or replace many aspects of a lawyer's job, including both fee-earning and business processes;
- Clients demand and expect more speedy, accurate, expert, creative, intuitive, and accessible legal advice;

- Pressure is growing both from within law firms (and in-house teams) and from clients to respond to the demand for customer-designed services;
- Technology-related projects that are both user and client-centric need to be implemented successfully; and
- In the long term, everyone will be using these kinds of technologies, despite the fact that AI deployment in the legal world has a last mile problem, comments Rick Seabrook, managing director of Neota Logic, Europe.

Four aspects of legal services

As we witness the evolution of AI and its take-up in the world at large, I predict we will experience a more measured approach and gradual warming to the evolution of AI in the legal world, which will then lead to a tsunami deployment within a couple of years – similar to the social media warming but on synthetic, exponential steroids. There will be AlphaLaw pioneers, just like there were social media pioneers.

Due to the deployment of smart tech, CC, AI, and robots in the legal ecosystem where lawyers, firms, general counsel, and clients are beginning to embrace such technologies, we're seeing that lawyering is increasingly becoming more productive, efficient, accurate, better quality, and less labour and time intensive, and the role of the lawyer is gradually shifting and changing.

There are, at present, several key providers of smart CC, AI, and robot technologies that relate to all aspects of legal services provision, and they deal with different aspects of the lawyer's role. If we break down a lawyer's tasks in a legal project from beginning to end, we find there is a technology that can handle the majority of these four tasks far more quickly and accurately than a human lawyer.

CC, AI, and robots are currently (and mainly) used and being considered for use in the legal ecosystem as a carthorse – for example, e-discovery, research, business processes, basic analytics or analysis, hypothesising, etc. – where they speed up much of the mundane elements of legal work. For example:

- Big Law American firm BakerHostetler is the first licensee of ROSS, hailed as the world's first AI lawyer and a 'very smart artificial co-worker', which interacts using natural language and is used for bankruptcy-related legal research matters. ROSS (owned by

ROSS Intelligence Inc.), an AI product and service resulting from the use of Apple's slick Siri voice capabilities and IBM Watson's cognitive computing prowess, was in the development and pilot stage throughout 2015 but will now be a huge boon for lawyers, law firms, and clients;

- BLP has been using RAVN ACE (applied cognitive engine) AI technology in the UK since 2015 in its real estate department and commercial practices. Used for 'deep research' and processing, such as extracting specific pieces of information from large documents, the technology has been nicknamed Lonald by BLP associates who welcome the machine as being more efficient, productive, and accurate than they could possibly be. Lonald is due to be 'rolled-out' in all BLP departments over the next three years in an attempt to boost efficiency and improve the morale of its lawyers;
- The first Magic Circle firm to go public with the use of AI, Linklaters has also signed a deal with technology provider RAVN Systems, the details of which remain confidential. The *Financial Times* also reveals the company has developed Verifi, a computer programme that can sift through 14 European and UK regulatory registers to check client names for banks. The company said it could 'process thousands of names overnight';
- Riverview Law launched KIM – an AI virtual assistant – in January 2016, followed up in April the same year with an AI triage of managed services technology and an AI platform, a huge advantage for general counsel and law departments in corporations, and for clients of all company sizes;
- Pinsent Masons has developed a programme that reads and analyses clauses in loan agreements. Its TermFrame system helps guide its lawyers through transactions and points them towards the correct precedents at each stage of a process; and
- Hodge, Jones & Allen has been working with academics from University College London to create software that assesses the merits of personal injury cases since 2014/15.

All of these AI systems and computer programmes handle large quantities of structured and unstructured data, and assist with the process, management, research, and reasoning elements related to legal issues. Two years ago they were not even in play in the legal market, though they were on the horizon.

Time equals money

For entrepreneurial lawyers and law firms, CC, AI, and robots also provide the opportunity to rethink legal service offerings. For example, with RAVN's AI technology, a law firm that has a client with tens of thousands of employment contracts across the world could offer the existing client an 'employment contract analysis' in relation to risk and compliance issues (for example, when there is new regulation or when the law bites). RAVN can configure a robot that will tell the firm or client what their exposure is. Providing this kind of legal service would have been impossible previously due to the disproportionate spend in time and cost; however, RAVN takes a routine, cognitive process (traditionally undertaken by junior lawyers labouring over a long period of time, usually months) and transforms it into an automated process, which can be completed in a matter of minutes or hours. Consequently, something that is incredibly difficult for a human to do but that a robot finds very easy could be offered as a valuable new legal service. RAVN is currently in the process of developing a whitepaper on the potential of deploying AI technologies in the legal world, which should prove highly informative and helpful to curious minds.

This has been, and is, our current and main level of understanding, thinking, application, and deployment of smart tech, CC, and AI in the legal industry. And yet, a search for 'AI in law' produces 105,000 results in the news section alone of Google's vast index. From the web as a whole, 25,900,000 results can be found, meaning there is appetite, curiosity, and interest in searching for how AI and the robots may be of use in the legal ecosystem more widely.

These technologies could, to some extent, be used in every aspect of legal service provision, not just the mundane 'everyday' legal matters of 'doing' but also the more lucrative area of 'thinking' and 'advisory'.

Evolving legal artificial intelligence from carthorse to racehorse

Law firms have only just begun to think of using AI technologies as a racehorse, not a carthorse. Global players Taylor Wessing and Norton Rose Fulbright have each independently collaborated with software and AI developer Neota Logic in creating AI apps, named TW: navigate PSC App and ContractorCheck respectively.

Taylor Wessing's app, introduced in April 2016, acts as a guide and adviser with respect to the recent changes to the Companies Act, where there is now a requirement for companies to identify and name persons of significant control in their returns to Companies House. Norton Rose

Fulbright describes its app, introduced in late 2015/early 2016, as 'an innovative tool designed to help organisations accurately characterise their people to manage risk, so that contracts truly reflect an individual's contractor or employee status. This smart identification tool has been tailored to apply the key characterisation indicators across multiple jurisdictions.'

Both firms have rethought how they deliver specific aspects of lawyering and are beginning to focus on racehorse elements of lawyering, which are the high-end, intellectual capital, reasoning, and judgement elements usually locked away in a lawyer's mind. Neota Logic works in collaboration with law firms, and elicits knowledge and experience from a lawyer to then 'brain dump' that information into software. Algorithms are then created which respond to the client or prospect without the need for a person. In theory it means a lawyer or law firm could serve hundreds or even thousands of clients, prospects, or queries seamlessly while they sleep – and get paid for it.

Each bespoke AI app mimics and replaces what a lawyer does in relation to the process, reasoning, and judgement elements (the knowledge and experience aspects) of a lawyer's specific area of law. For example, a lawyer will ask a series of questions to a client who will reply with their answers: throughout, the lawyer pulls on their knowledge and experience of the law and provides the client with the answers they seek. This kind of AI technology is beginning to prove popular for:

- Online compliance;
- Online legal assessment; and
- Providing online documents and advice solutions.

Using this kind of technology is also proving to be a smart way of marketing, creating, and building relationships with new and existing clients.

Inviolable lawyers

Currently, there are automated, cognitive computing (CC), and AI systems that support lawyers and which replace lawyers. Nevertheless, as machines become more intelligent and lawyers become more comfortable in deploying and working with these systems, it is inevitable that the machine will make a switch from carthorse to racehorse functionality, and will replace more and more of a human lawyer's key roles in relation to the four elements of legal services provision (commoditisation, research, reasoning, and judgement), edging into the realm where lawyers think they are immune and untouchable.

But they are neither immune nor untouchable. No area of law, including corporate, commercial, intellectual property, employment, property, tax, bankruptcy, family, or litigation will escape the march of the machine. Within the legal ecosystem, we will see AI evolve from CC (which demands a significant amount of data) and mimicking the human brain to iterative intelligence and design algorithms (rules-based programming and self-learning where the AI or robot learns for itself); then, eventually, artificial general intelligence will come about via the Google Brain, White House BRAIN Initiative (Brain Research through Advancing Innovative Neurotechnologies), or DARPA AI projects – possibly in around 15 to 20 years' time.

It is not impossible that we will witness a world champion AI lawyer, not unlike a world champion AI player in Go, an AI Poker player, within the next few years. The rate of technological development and AI innovation is exponential. Accordingly, the likelihood is that many aspects (but not all) of lawyering as we know it now can and will be done with little human intervention within five to 10 years. This prediction is in line with the global research suggesting that, within 10 years, 57 per cent of blue-collar and white-collar work, globally, will be replaced by automation, AI, or robots.

So, you have two choices: the first is to embrace the rise of smart CC, AI, and robot technologies; management may be responsible for providing the environment to facilitate change and innovation, but the responsibility to embrace change rests with each and every lawyer in our firms or legal departments. The second is to ignore emerging technologies, do nothing, and get left behind.

Paper-pusher pushout

Another prediction is that massively overpaid paper-pushers will be side-lined within one to three years. If you understand that smart AI technology is not here to replace you (well, not immediately) but to make you a better lawyer, and to force you to use your instinct, emotional intelligence, and capitalise on your mind, then you have made the first step in future-proofing your career and business. The brave new legal eco-system will require 'algorithmic angels', in which the primary lawyerly role will be:

- To interpret that the AI or robot is correct about the law; and
- To provide a supportive relationship to clients and general counsel.

There will only be three kinds of human worker or lawyer within the next 10 years when the machines rule:

- Those with high-end emotional intelligence and relationship skills;
- Those who provide support to the machine systems; or
- Unemployed.

With the exception of those firms that have already gone public in relation to the deployment of AI systems (some of which were named earlier), companies and firms already using or considering using these technologies include a selection of those from:

- The Big Four accountancy firms;
- Magic Circle firms;
- The top 50; and
- Those outside the top 50, i.e. those with distinct specialities that aim to use AI to win new clients and compete with the top 50. These types of private practice include real estate, immigration, pensions, and finance.

Renovating private practice

Rethinking legal services may also entail rethinking what type of business of law will be most suitable going forward. Law firm consultant George Beaton recently released a fascinating piece of research on why 'Big Law' should start to reinvent itself due to the mix of legal service providers predicted to be in the market in 10 years' time.[1] These types of private practice include Big Law; traditional or remade traditional law; New Law; standalone automated legal service providers (for example, Riverview Law); and in-house general counsels. The findings predict that a staggering 50 per cent of Big Law and traditional firms will be 'remade' and will lose significant market share to the other types of businesses within the next decade.

Accordingly, my advice, as ever, is to future-proof yourself and your business now. It is inevitable that smart tech, AI, and robots do – and will continue to – support us positively in our current roles, but eventually they may replace lawyers entirely in carrying out particular tasks once AI exceeds human lawyerly intelligence; we're talking a handful of months or years here, not decades.

Ask yourself the following:

- Can you afford not to be prepared for the time when 'the machine' evolves and inevitably does your fee earning and performs business processes quicker and more accurately, more creatively, and smarter than you can?
- Can you afford not to embrace the machine, when your existing and new competitors are already using it, or about to? and
- Can you afford not to deploy CC and AI technologies when your existing and new clients are beginning to expect some form of these systems as part of a legal service offering?

If you ask me today what I believe the next 'big thing' in legal is going to be, my reply is as follows:

My human brain is available for hire now on a one-to-one basis, but in the near future – say, within five years – everyone on the planet (potentially seven billion people; nine billion by 2050) and Mars (if Elon Musk et al are successful) and beyond will be able to help themselves to it (for an adjusted, volume-based, significantly reduced fee, or in some instances free of charge where I see the value in creating goodwill and building a client base for another premium service), in the form of an AI app and available online (omnipresent 24 hours a day, seven days a week, 365 days a year) via an AI platform in the cloud.

I am not complacent about what my role will be in the ensuing months and years. Nor should you be. Do not assume that smart technology, AI, and the robots will not be able to do significant elements of your job, even the complex stuff. Prepare for the possibility that they could and most likely will.

A version of this chapter was first published as a two-part article in Solicitors Journal *(31 May and 6 June 2016).*

References

1. Beaton, G. and Kaschner, I. *Remaking Law Firms: Why & How?* ABA, 2016.

Chapter 4:
The missing 'E' in legal innovation

By John Alber, futurist at the International Legal Technology Association

Innovation talk

Cruise through the business press these days, or any number of legal industry resources, and you'll find the word 'innovation' coming up often. It's become a theme of our age, and no less in law than in any other discipline.

Especially since the Great Recession, law firm clients, too, have taken up the cause of innovation – demanding that their law firms become radically more innovative in terms of pricing, unbundling, service delivery, and a host of other areas. Indeed, through organisations like the Corporate Legal Operations Consortium (CLOC) and the Association of Corporate Counsel (ACC), clients are banding together precisely to foster innovation in the firms that serve them. They're 'unionising' around these subjects, trying to accomplish by joint action what individual persuasion has failed to do over the years.

And some firms are listening. Big Law firms have recently been racing to appoint innovation partners or chief innovation officers, to field innovation committees, to feature innovation in their strategic plans, and even to create innovation-focused business units. Mid-sized and small firms, too, have heard the call and are talking up the need to innovate at partner retreats, conferences, and legal network meetings.

But is all the innovation talk inside law firms enough to initiate the wave of innovation that clients seem to want? Are we truly witnessing the advance guard of transformation in how legal services are delivered?

The simple answer is no. Firms are using the words, but even the most vocal are not taking the kinds of concrete, disciplined steps that truly innovative companies in other business sectors undertake on the way to radically innovative solutions.

The shortfall is so profound, so unlike the kind of A-student effort that lawyers typically undertake in legal spheres, that it's as though lawyers can't even spell the word innovation. They are missing the most important letter. The letter 'E'.

Apple innovation

To understand the point here, we'll jump industries and talk about innovation in mobile devices – an area in which, over the last decade, we've witnessed real transformation at a level that affects each of us personally. And we'll also need to transport back in time to 2006 – one year before Apple's iPhone completely altered the market for cell phones and a dozen other portable devices.

Figure 1: The bestselling phone in 2006 was the Motorola RAZR...

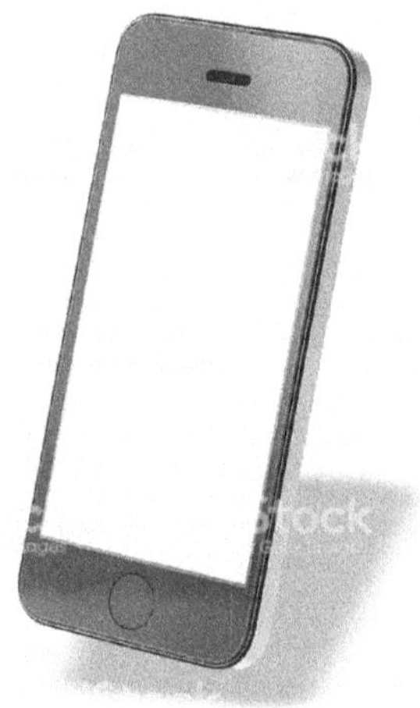

Figure 2: ...until Apple's iPhone upended the market

The bestselling phone in 2006 was the Motorola RAZR, a clamshell device that started out in 2004 as an expensive testament to Motorola's fashion sense. But, as Motorola dropped the price from $600 (a lot of money back then) to just a few hundred, consumers responded overwhelmingly, and Motorola found themselves with a huge success. They sold 130 million RAZRs over the life of the product. And that was a record.

How did the marketplace respond to RAZR? People marvelled at its 'thinness' and its 'elegance'. And that spawned a number of thin, elegant imitators. Here's what Avi Greengart, a prominent cellphone analyst for research firm Current Analysis said about all that:

> *'Fashion and thinness have become an overriding concern. Where in 2005 you might have had one or two phones that either were the RAZR or looked like it, in 2006 we now have a plethora of super-thin clamshell phones, including phones with spectacular feature sets.'*

Among the 'spectacular' features just included in the RAZR were a low-end MP3 player and a low-resolution camera. The tacked-on MP3 player was an attempt to take market share away from Apple's hugely successful iPod. Then along came Apple.

If we think about the first iPhone, we might mistake its real innovations. After all, its marvellous touch-screen interface and elegantly thin form factor did get mentioned a lot by consumers. They still do. Was Apple's success attributable simply to the fact that the iPhone out RAZRed the RAZR in terms of thinness and features?

That focus on appearance overlooks something fundamental about Apple's approach – about Apple's *process* for innovation. It was the process that shot the iPhone to the front of the market for mobile devices.

Apple pursued a completely different design course from everyone else in the cellular market. In contrast with others, which often used competing design teams, Apple used the very same design team throughout its design of the Newton, the iPod, the iPhone, and succeeding mobile products. Indeed, most of the designers of the original iPhone are still on the Apple design team.

And those designers steeped themselves in Apple's and Motorola's customer base. Not only did they poll them, but they engaged them on a much deeper level, conducting focus groups, following users around as they interacted with devices, doing everything short of a Vulcan mind meld to try to put themselves not just in the shoes of their customers, but in their hearts as well. Oh, and Apple was first to implement this requirement: each member of Apple's design team had to actually use the devices they designed. They became their own user base.

Apple's design team reported directly to Steve Jobs. In many ways, he was the head of the design team. No marketing or accounting considerations stood between the team and either consumers or Apple leadership. What the design team learned about their customers' lives got reported directly up to Jobs.

Both by virtue of their long continuity with the team and their intense engagement with customers, Apple's designers came to understand those customers' needs on a deeper level than even the customers themselves did. If you had asked RAZR customers what they wanted in a next generation phone, they would have said thinner, or maybe a keyboard. Not an iPhone.

Apple's foremost lesson from its deep dive into how customers used mobile devices had nothing to do with customer-favourite feature sets or form factors. It didn't focus on thinness or fashion. Rather, it learned that the multiplication of devices, features, and functions was imposing a significant data management burden on users. Keeping track of all your music, contacts, appointments, photographs, emails, texts, messages, and other items across a range of devices was difficult for even the most savvy users. And utterly maddening for everyone else.

Thus, it wasn't Apple's elegant touch screen or polished case that caused the iPhone to surge to first among all mobile phones in just one year. It was that deep understanding of what users truly needed. Apple vaulted to the forefront in the mobile device market because, more than any other company in the market space, it was able to *empathise* with its customers and act on that understanding.

Empathy is the E in innovation. And it allowed Apple to sell as many iPhones in a quarter as Motorola sold RAZRs over the entire history of the device. By the way, it's no accident that Apple's designers are now attuned to another mobile device: the automobile. That design decision is the product of deep empathy as well.

Design Thinking

The techniques that allowed Apple to conceptualise and deliver the iPhone, and that have served other product innovators so well, have been studied and written about extensively. While Apple itself has been unusually guarded about its methods, others who worked closely with Steve Jobs have distilled Apple's methods and elaborated upon them.

Those techniques, now often referred to under the mantle of 'Design Thinking', have been exploding out of the design disciplines and into business, even into a small corner of the law, because they can accomplish more than is possible or likely with traditional business – or legal – methodologies.

Tim Brown, CEO of global innovation firm IDEO (with which Apple worked closely on a number of designs) and a leading proponent of Design Thinking, describes the revolution inherent in Design Thinking this way:

> *'Design Thinking is a human-centered approach to innovation that draws from the designer's toolkit to integrate the needs of people, the possibilities of technology and the requirements for business success.'*

Stanford University's Design School, which has become an open-source epicentre for Design Thinking in Silicon Valley and beyond, has distilled the elements of Design Thinking into these five tasks, as illustrated in Figure 3.

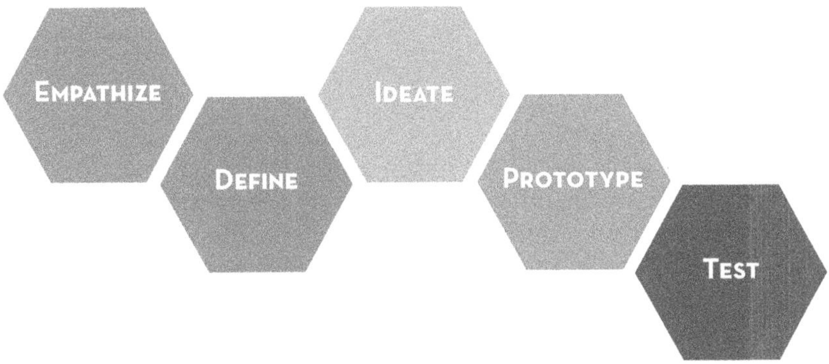

Figure 3: The Stanford d.School Design Thinking process[1]

A business using Design Thinking methods first does the sort of deep dive into customer hearts and minds that Apple did with its users. That is the Empathise phase. Then the problem is defined – as Apple did in identifying data management as a principal concern. Then ideas are spun out. But not one perfect idea at a time. Dozens of them. Even hundreds. Those are prioritised and the best of them go quickly and cheaply to some sort of prototype phase – even to paper prototypes. And those are tested with users. Then the process is repeated. Over and over and over. Iteration is essential to design. Which is to say that mistakes are also essential to design.

If we think about how most businesses, including law, design solutions to problems, we can recognise that most use far fewer than five steps in the process. Indeed, I would argue that the famously ovine legal sector uses just one: buy or try what someone else has bought or tried, and test it to see if it works. That sort of approach is certainly the genesis of many technology failures in the legal sector. They fail because they are purchasing decisions, uninformed by any of the prior design work necessary to assure that purchases are solving real and immediate problems.

It's not surprising that law firms and others short circuit process in doing service design. Empathy, the most important element of this human-centred approach to innovation, is something utterly outside the toolset given lawyers in law school. Empathy goes beyond simply trying to understand a problem. It asks you to put yourself in the shoes of the person who will use your product or service, and to try to understand that person in ways that transcend logic, that draw upon intuition and emotion as well.

Design Thinking recognises the first-level importance of the emotional content of a successful design. When we think of traditional value propositions, we often bring to mind some notion of utility. This product or service will accomplish a certain thing. Lawyers think like that. We will provide you with advice, and it will be correct.

But the most successful designs go beyond mere utility. If you buy a Tesla, the automaker promises that you will receive the safest transportation in the world, that you will be transported in a sumptuous surround, that you will feel pampered, affluent, intelligent. In other words, the design of a Tesla is loaded with emotional content. So too with the iPhone. Its design is a response to what was often a visceral frustration with complexity. Its beautiful simplicity is directed at emotion at least as much as at aesthetics.

Clients have been telling us for years that they want more than utility in their law firms. One of the most common complaints in annual surveys about lawyers is that they take no time to understand their clients' businesses. That complaint certainly relates to the utility of advice – abstract advice is less valuable than that given in a specific business context. But the complaint also has just as much emotional content as a 'you don't pay enough attention to me' statement in any other human relationship.

A new model?

What would law practice look like if it began to incorporate Design Thinking principles? What has come to be called NewLaw certainly furnishes some examples. Rocket Lawyer and Legal Zoom have recognised and responded to the deep frustration inherent in constituencies that have been priced out of traditional legal markets. Their services are easy to use, inexpensive, and for simple transactions often at least as accurate as the services provided by high street generalists. A legal consumer's reaction to the extensive document automation at the heart of those services might approximate that of the first iPhone users: 'You mean I can do all this in one place? And it's easy?'

The lawyer response to such enthusiasm is often to say those tools are meant for consumer-grade legal problems. They can't possibly apply to more complex legal issues. That, unfortunately, is a typical problem-focused lawyer analysis – the kind Design Thinking circumvents. But a deeper dive into the client psyche would reveal that easier and cheaper are two of the foremost desires of clients – even sophisticated corporate clients. Lawyers are hard to reach, often unresponsive, and impose high costs on every second of interaction. Design Thinking starts with desires like that.

NewLaw Design Thinking has in fact extended well beyond consumer legal transactions. For example, we tend to think of 'contract automation' solutions as manifestations of AI or machine intelligence simply being redirected towards legal problems. AI may be the technology that underlies the latest contract automation products, but the fact that the problem – which has been sitting under lawyers' noses for decades – was identified at all is a clue to the existence of Design Thinking. Someone plumbed deeply the frustration and complexity inherent in managing the large numbers of contracts a global company enters into annually. And we see, as a consequence of that inquiry, the kind of iterative design/redesign cycles in the marketplace that are the markers of real Design Thinking. As with the iPhone, when the empathy phase is done correctly, market uptake can be dramatic. And that has happened in the contract automation market.

Perhaps the most fundamental example of Design Thinking in law occurs almost completely outside the legal sector. Blockchain technology – the peer-to-peer network infrastructure that made possible cryptocurrencies like Bitcoin – was designed to support 'smart contracts'. These effect the tracking and transfer of digitals assets in ways that almost completely circumvent traditional legal processes. Smart contracts exist in code, not on paper, are self-enforcing without need for courts or other trusted intermediaries, and operate with orders of magnitude more efficiency, and less cost than traditional contracting processes. They are a redefinition of both money and law and an attempt at solving frustrations and inefficiencies that have long plagued traditional contracting processes. The only one who could love a traditional asset transfer – one that depended on reams of paper, inscrutable prose, antediluvian court systems, and curmudgeonly, expensive, and fussy guild workers – would be someone paid by the hour for all that trouble. No one else loves it. And blockchain is the result.

Those, such as lawyer/computer scientist Nick Szabo, who did the early work on blockchain and smart contracting, were doing a classic Design Thinking deep dive into the problems of digital commerce. What has emerged is just as iterative as the iPhone. Blockchain is certainly still in early prototype and testing stages. But billions of dollars of our clients' money is being invested to multiply the iterations until contracting is as unrecognisable to us as iPhones would have been to early 2000s cell phone users.

How many other components of our legal infrastructure are susceptible to the kind of redesign undertaken by blockchain? Certainly more than most lawyers imagine. But the threat of being designed out of existence has some firms taking a harder look at Design Thinking, and incorporating its principles into service redesign. For example, King Wood Mallesons has instituted annual 'design weeks' during which lawyers, staff, and clients take the kind of deep empathy dive contemplated by Design Thinking and try to arrive at radical new ways of delivering legal services. Other firms are beginning to send lawyers and staff off to Design Thinking 'bootcamps' such as those offered by the Stanford D School.

But can firms do enough, soon enough, to participate in the revolution that seems certain to transform the law in coming decades? Here's a key differentiator between lawyer thinking and Design Thinking. Lawyers and business people want answers to questions like this. But there is no one answer to these problems. To arrive at something optimal – to an iPhone-like solution – we will have to dive deep, define goals, spin out ideas, and then prototype. And fail, then revise, then cycle through the whole process again.

Empathy, coupled with a disposition to experiment and a tolerance for failure, are the hallmarks of Design Thinking. Those are disciplines designers take for granted. But they are disciplines yet to be added to the lawyer toolkit.

It may be that enough lawyers can begin to master these disciplines, can take a real hand in the redesign of legal services that is already underway, so as to have real impact on the result. Or it may be that redesign will be left to others. In the end, we can't say what a redesigned law practice will look like. We can only say that the best answers will have been designed in all the best senses of the word. And good design is always a surprise.

Reference

1. Resources created by Hasso Plattner Institute of Design at Stanford and licensed under a Creative Commons Attribution-Non-Commercial-ShareAlike 3.0 Unported License. For more information, see: https://dschool-old.stanford.edu/groups/dresources/.

Chapter 5:
The evolving legal talent pool

By Debbie Epstein Henry, founder of DEH Consulting, Speaking, Writing; co-founder of Bliss Lawyers

Twenty years ago, a lawyer's career path was linear and unforgiving. Particularly in the large law firm environment, the expectation was that if you wanted to succeed, you needed to stay on track. That translated to no career breaks, no alternative schedules, and no deviations from substantive practice that would make a lawyer appear anything other than committed and focused on career progression.

Women were the first to challenge the traditional model, many of whom were the 'canaries in the coal mine', frustrated that the partnership track would not give them the flexibility to build a career and a life at the same time. Countless women found the partnership track untenable and left the profession. Among those who stayed, many were stigmatised and 'mommy-tracked'. And for some of those women who remained on the traditional track, it meant foregoing marriage and/or children to conform and succeed on the only path to equity.

That rigid path has begun to erode, and those with less linear career paths may no longer need to be casualties of the system. However, it's not because the legal profession has suddenly gone squishy. Instead, powerful market drivers are propelling the shift and do not appear to be going away anytime soon; nor should they. These drivers are principally the economy and associated changes in client demands. Other contributors are demographic shifts that are impacting lawyers' career trajectories, and in turn the receptivity to alternative career paths.

With respect to clients, they are no longer shy in communicating their pressures and changed expectations.[1] Given the volatility of the market, in-house lawyers face headcount constraints and shrinking budgets, yet they also expect to do more work internally. They demand more predictability in their fee structures from their outside providers, and seek more alternative fees, value, and risk sharing. They resist paying for junior lawyer training, and they seek more flexibility, creativity, and collaboration in their legal service providers. Additionally, they push for disaggregation of work and technology adoption and they are more solicitous of alternative legal models.

Parallel with these increased client pressures and expectations are the demographic shifts in how millennials and baby boomers build and exit their careers. Millennials, generally less concerned with longevity in their jobs, are more open to non-linear careers. They also seek more flexibility in the way in which they work, and they push the work/life agenda in gender-neutral ways for reasons beyond family.

Meanwhile, many baby boomers don't like the way their bank accounts look as they approach retirement. They also find their children returning home after college in greater numbers, leading to more expenses than they had envisioned. These factors and others have led baby-boomer lawyers at the senior arc of their careers to phase into retirement, and work flexible or reduced hours for a period of years rather than retire outright like many of their predecessors. The visible example of these revered leaders in the profession working differently helps to destigmatise flexible working as well as less traditional careers.

Beyond the millennials and baby boomers, over the last decade, lawyers with less linear careers are being judged less harshly, thanks in large part to the mass layoffs of lawyers in the great recession of the late 2000s and its aftermath. With less certainty in the market came more acceptance of résumé gaps. This helps other lawyers who find themselves unemployed due to relocations for a spouse's job (including military spouses who are transplanted to different geographies on a regular basis) and those lawyers negatively impacted by firm and corporate mergers and reorganisations as well as general and widespread downsizing and outsourcing initiatives.

In a virtuous cycle, once the market became more inviting to lawyers in transition, in turn, these lawyers became more willing to articulate their true desires to work differently. The erratic market has also helped some lawyers develop a greater appetite for risk, recognising that their jobs were not as secure as they might have thought. Lawyers' increased willingness to work in secondment roles (temporary engagements) and for virtual firms, as well as for other NewLaw[2] models, also exemplify the shifting roles of lawyers in the market. Some of these lawyers seek alternative paths due to involuntary layoffs, relocations, desires to reinvent or expand their industry experience, and to supplement solo practices and gain in-house experience. Others seek non-traditional roles in legal settings like project or knowledge management. This trend towards alternative paths reinforces the predictions of experts that future growth in legal jobs is in non-traditional roles like legal process engineers, technologists, and process analysts.[3]

Ultimately, clients' needs will drive lawyers' career paths. And when it comes to talent, clients want better alignment between lawyers' work, skills, and seniority, and the fees that are charged. For law firms, this translates into bringing more candour to the career progression process and creating viable alternative paths to equity partner. While many firms have created different titles for lawyers beyond equity partner – e.g., non-equity partner, counsel, senior attorney, staff attorney – lawyers in these positions are often side-lined, with little chance of an entrée back to the equity partner track.

For law firms to remain competitive in the talent sphere, they should instead create more fluidity among the different titles and roles, allowing lawyers to flow from one function to another, and to ramp up and down their practice, assuming their skills warrant promotion and their emerging roles are consistent with the business needs of the firm.[4] In addition to allowing a return to equity track for lawyers who are poised for the transition back, each of the other roles at firms, along with equity, should still have progression tracks and valued paths. This would allow firms to attract and retain a more diverse pool of lawyers and better align the lawyers' contributions with the fees charged to clients.

While there is today a greater openness to lawyers with jig-jagged experience, many legal employers have yet to fully appreciate the value of attracting and retaining lawyers who wish to create patchwork careers. Many law firms and legal service providers have yet to realise that this is really what clients want. Indeed, clients are demanding more choice and flexibility, and by affording lawyers the ability to work differently, employers can better serve clients' needs at the varying levels and rates that clients want. For law firms, this means creating more hospitable workplaces where lawyers contribute at different levels, and firms bill these lawyers out to their clients at a greater range of predictable rates.

To make law firms more hospitable, the focus also needs to be on supporting both male and female lawyers over their full career span. This means setting reasonable hours and protecting vacations, as well as instituting generous gender-neutral policies involving parental leave, childcare, eldercare, flexible and reduced hours, re-entry back to the profession, and phased retirement. Creating a more hospitable workplace that cultivates lawyers who bring true value to clients requires law firms and other legal service providers to invest in their talent as people – not simply as lawyers. This means going beyond training in substantive expertise, and working to cultivate lawyers' skills in leadership, sponsorship, and networking, among other areas.

Bottom line is that lawyers' lives are not linear and therefore legal careers need not be either. Legal employers who ultimately win the talent war will be those who embrace the evolving talent pool, support lawyers at each stage of their career trajectories, and ensure that these lawyers are meeting client needs in an ever-changing market.

References

1. See Henry, D.E., Rabinowitz, S.S. and Berger, G.A. *Finding Bliss: Innovative Legal Models for Happy Clients & Happy Lawyers*, ABA, 2015. (pp. 11–36)
2. NewLaw is defined as 'any strategy, structure, model, process or way of delivering legal services that represents a significantly different approach to the creation or provision of legal services than what the legal profession traditionally has employed'. Jordan Furlong and Sean Larkan of Edge International, '*A Brief Inventory of NewLaw in Australia*' at ALPMA, A Survival Guide for Legal Practice Managers, 25 August 2014.
3. See generally, Susskind, R. *Tomorrow's Lawyers: An Introduction to Your Future*, Oxford University Press, 2013.
4. Henry, Rabinowitz, and Berger, *Finding Bliss*. (pp. 85–97)

Chapter 6:
Rethinking pricing and profitability

By Michael Roster, co-chair of the Association of Corporate Counsel's Value Challenge steering committee; previously managing partner of Morrison & Foerster's Los Angeles office and GC of Stanford University

Both inside and outside counsel in recent years have been focusing again on value. That in turn has led to discussion of the three targets set forth in the Association of Corporate Counsel's Value Challenge:

- *Reduce total legal cost* (inside and outside lawyers combined) by a specific amount, typically 25 per cent or more, which most companies are achieving;
- *Provide high predictability* such as fixed pricing by task, matter, or portfolio, as well as in how matters are handled; and
- *Improve outcomes.*

These changes are now forcing firms and clients to figure out: How do you price a matter? And how does a law firm sustain its profitability in this new environment?

The historical problem

Until 30 or so years ago, clients and firms worldwide actually managed legal services based on value through the use of fixed prices, retainers, contingency fees, and the like. Monthly, semi-annual, or even annual bills often simply read 'for services rendered', but the law firm had long-standing ties to the corporate client and gave a lot of careful thought as to what that number should be.

It's when firms and clients started pricing legal services by the hour that things went off track. This counterproductive methodology became established when law firms started using computers to keep track of their work, in-house lawyers decided they wanted to see the computer printouts as the sole determinant of price and value, and law firms that initially resisted this approach soon made a science of it instead.

Without well-meaning people realising it, the billable hour created highly perverse incentives for law firms to keep increasing their cost of production. This is contrary to what most manufacturers and service providers do, which is to continually look for ways to reduce the cost of production while significantly improving the quality of the product. Just look at what has happened with mobile phones, flat screen televisions, even automobiles. Same for basic dental services, tax preparation services, and other similar professional services.

The hourly system also created an incentive to maximise inefficiencies. Law firm managers started boasting about their efforts to get rid of non-billing support staff even though these support staff were highly efficient for activities such as preparing and updating drafts, assembling files, etc. The result was that we had lawyers billing $250-an-hour or more doing the work of a secretary.

Put another way, imagine if you were going to add a room to your house and your contractor was going to bill you by the hour, plus the marked-up cost of materials. Your contractor would have little if any incentive to be efficient. She or he would be incentivised instead to use people who worked slowly but were priced high ('I only use the best of the best'). She or he would mark up materials as much as the market (you) could bear. She or he would have no incentive to figure out ways to do the job faster, more efficiently, and yet with higher quality. And she or he would get rid of back office people who did things like purchasing and scheduling and instead would have the front-line construction crew billing for this same work, and by the hour.

Use of market data to determine pricing

As we go back to value-based pricing, how do law firms and clients determine the right price for a matter? The market is one factor. Increasingly, there are databases that show, based on averages but often with greater granularity when desired, what every type of task or matter is costing in specific legal markets.

Much of the data comes from the widespread adoption in recent years of electronic billing. By processing huge numbers of electronic bills that contain huge amounts of information, the service providers also gained access to highly reliable data that could be aggregated and then used for an entirely new product and service.

Some service providers can even show what a specific type of task or matter is likely to cost firm to firm and, in many instances, can even drill down to show which lawyers and practice groups at any given firm are more efficient as compared to competing practice groups and firms. There are deficiencies in this type of data, at least so far. For example, a lawyer is deemed less efficient by many of these service providers if he or she shows block billing such as billing 14 hours in a single day on a single matter. In reality, sometimes that is a sign that an attorney was padding the hours, but in other instances it is penalising a highly capable lawyer who worked single-mindedly on a specific matter day and night.

Another approach, within the confines of the antitrust laws, is for clients themselves to start developing databases that show the cost of legal services for specific types of tasks or matters, in specific geographic regions, at specific levels of difficulty, and even broken down by which law firms, judges, government entities, or opposing counsel were involved.

Many trade associations also have long published data for their specific industries. For example, what percentage of revenue is devoted by companies in the same industry for legal services? When I started as general counsel at Stanford, I found one such study done years earlier by the national college and university trade group. That study showed a certain percentage of revenue was spent, on average, by private universities and a different percentage by public universities. When I called my colleagues around the country, most were not aware of this survey but when they looked at their own numbers quickly confirmed that their school was almost exactly in line with the benchmark.

Knowing my benchmark for my industry was very helpful for me as a general counsel. It allowed me to know if our total legal spend (internal and external combined) was in the ballpark. Once I knew that, I was then able to make separate decisions about whether we were making the best use of our total expenditures for legal services, again both in-house and outside combined.

Matrix budget

Which leads to another approach for determining pricing and, over time, law firm profitability.

At Stanford we created what I called a matrix budget. On the horizontal axis of an Excel spreadsheet we listed all of our relevant cost centres, and on the vertical axis we listed all of the substantive legal areas we were using (environmental, land use, etc.). That created something like 100 active cells where we then inputted our actual or estimated total spend (again, internal and external combined) in the prior year for each type of substantive legal service for each cost centre.

In many instances, we readily saw that some units within the university or the medical centre were consuming high cost legal services when in fact there was little if any legal exposure. We also saw areas where we were devoting a lot of expensive legal resources to problems or compliance that could be better handled by people with different and considerably less expensive backgrounds and skills.

The three Es

This budgeting and pricing project took into account what I called the three Es, and law firms and general counsel might take these items into account as they develop methods for determining price.

1. Expertise

I knew from my law firm days as a managing partner and as a practice group head that our value as outside counsel was largely based on our expertise. We often could give a client an answer to a complex question in a matter of minutes or hours, whereas competitors would put a large number of lawyers on the project, spend hours and days researching it all, and then deliver a memo that might or might not be relevant or right.

Because we were handling such a high number of matters, most being somewhat routine but many being bet the company, we knew both the nuts and bolts of most issues but we also had the information and skills needed in bet-the-company types of matters.

2. Expense

The cost of a specific task, matter, or portfolio is obviously important. In the Stanford project, each of our partner law firms was assigned several substantive portfolios (environmental, HR, medical regulatory, intellectual property, real estate, etc.) at a fixed price. The portfolios included both counselling and dispute resolution/litigation so there was a strong built-in incentive for firms to keep us out of trouble. The goal was for firms to deploy and be paid for their expertise, not their hours. At the end of the first year, our total legal costs were reduced by $1 million a year and at the end of five years we had half the litigation we had had the prior decade.

Moreover, we were seeing major benefits not only with what we were paying for legal services, but also the reputational costs that typically arise with disputes. Plus management was spending much less time on legal matters, something they clearly appreciated.

3. Elasticity

The third E stands for elasticity, something general counsel need to keep in mind and an important factor for law firms in their pricing.

There are many significant advantages to in-house legal departments. We in-house lawyers know the client well, we are in tune with corporate cultures and priorities, if managed correctly our costs are lower than outside counsel, and our managers appreciate the continuity of the lawyers involved.

There also are costs, however, to such a system, including a lack of elasticity. A company's legal requirements may change year to year, but a fixed internal system usually can't shift its in-house lawyers to areas that are significantly different year to year. A tax lawyer, for example, can't readily become an intellectual property litigator if that becomes the new priority. Also, making a reduction in force is difficult both legally and psychologically.

On the other hand, when a company makes effective use of outside counsel, there are no obstacles to shifting what substantive resources are needed at any given time, and with what level of experience. Likewise, if a specific law firm attorney isn't performing satisfactorily, the client can simply tell the firm to assign someone else.

The benefits of this type of elasticity should have a bearing on the overall pricing of the services obtained from outside counsel, or at least when making the classic 'make or buy' decision to do something in-house versus buy it from outside service providers.

Multi-disciplinary practices

As both inside and outside counsel look more closely at outcomes, pricing, and profitability, the concept of multi-disciplinary practice groups will become something to consider.

Over the past 20 to 30 years, both inside and outside counsel may have been too quick to treat nearly every problem as a *legal* problem. We lawyers adopted the concept that every problem somehow can be solved with lots of legal effort.

Fifteen years ago, there were heated debates within the American

Bar Association and elsewhere about the emerging threats of so-called multi-disciplinary practices. A leader in developing multi-disciplinary services was the now-defunct Arthur Andersen that was building a true law firm outside the US and doing significant crossovers of legal with other professional skills worldwide, including in the US. In recent years, virtually all of the major US accounting firms have been developing similar processes, but staying under the radar as they do so.

A few years ago, a long-time friend of mine, the owner and CEO of a major food processor in Europe, said to me: 'Lawyers, oh, we don't use them anymore.' Most of his legal exposures are in the workforce plus health and safety, and he then gave me the name of a multi-disciplinary practice entity he now uses. They write his employment and other manuals, as they do for a large number of other companies. They train his senior managers and his workforce. When they see patterns emerging as a result of their extensive work for a broad range of clients, on their own they modify the manuals, the training, and the compliance audits.

'Oh yes', my friend said, 'and if we get sued, which is very seldom now, they have some lawyers who take care of it'. He said this almost as an afterthought, which in reality is how it should be.

Not only have my friend's legal issues been significantly reduced, but he has the benefit of a fixed line item in his annual budget for what used to be a large unknown. On top of that, this same service provider now offers an optional insurance policy to cover any settlements and verdicts, which can give my friend even greater predictability in his annual budgeting.

The point is, as law firms move to an outcomes-based approach for pricing, they are going to need to look at dividing client matters into their constituent parts, determine what are the proper skills needed for each part, and somehow offer a turnkey approach that is competitively priced. Doing it by the hour and solely with lawyers will be a competitive disaster. Finding a way to offer a great service at a fixed price, and then working internally to increase profitability via the use of differing skills and improved processes, will be essential.

That also means shifting to a business model where the firm is rewarded for keeping a client out of trouble, versus the past business model that puts a premium on clients having troubles.

It's going to be a painful transition, but if the next generations of law firm partners and general counsel are thinking clearly, this is their future. And a rewarding one at that.

Chapter 7:
A new business model for a sustainable future

By Martyn Caplan, founder and director of Lawyers Inc.

Lawyers Inc. was formed following careful consideration as to why so many law firms were failing – and why so many lawyers were unhappy. Our starting point was to consider and understand why the traditional legal model was failing and fast becoming redundant.

The traditional legal model

The traditional legal firm was based upon the concept of perpetuity and the ultimate goal of becoming a *partner* in a law firm. A trainee would qualify as a solicitor, thereafter progress to becoming a salaried partner, and eventually introduce capital and become an equity partner. After many prosperous years, the equity partner would then retire, take out their capital with interest, and enjoy the benefits of a generous pension.

With a fluctuating financial economy and the instability or even collapse of many law firms, the above formula has become redundant. Increasingly lawyers began to take the view that it was not an attractive proposition to sign a partnership deed and thus become jointly and severally responsible for the bank borrowings, secondary lending, and property commitments of the legal firm.

In addition, if the practice failed they might potentially become responsible for redundancy payments, run-off insurance, and top-up insurance. Alternatively, if lawyers became directors of a limited liability partnership (LLP) or limited company they faced a potential personal financial liability if they were found to have been trading while insolvent.

Today's up-and-coming lawyers are understandably more reluctant to be subjected to the financial risks and pressures that come with taking an equitable stake in a legal practice. They more often appreciate and concur with the modern approach that a legal practice should be viewed as a business that happens to practice law. This is a very different view to the one that had been traditionally held of law firms somehow being aloof from and operating in an entirely separate way to other businesses, in a world where lawyers' expertise and knowledge was unquestionably in demand and where consumers didn't shop around.

Many younger lawyers began to question whether there was any real incentive to invest their career, or indeed their money, into their legal practice.

Potential threats to the financial stability and future of a legal practice

In England and Wales, the Solicitor's Regulation Authority (SRA) Code of Conduct 2011 (Principle 8) clearly recognises that a law firm is a business by providing that:

- The business must be run with sound financial and risk management;
- Budgets, expenditure, and cash flow must be controlled; and
- The financial stability and viability must be monitored in order to identify and mitigate any risks to the public.

Hence a compliance officer must be satisfied that the firm is making plans for the future, anticipating threats, and positioning itself to exploit opportunities to ensure continued viability and financial stability into the future. In addition, if there is no business plan for the future, banks may be reluctant to give continuing financial support and fee earners may decide to leave, which may result in an immediate drop in income for the firm.

When making an application to become an alternative business structure (ABS), the regulator requires a detailed three-year business plan before they will consider the application. There is no reason why a legal practice should depart from that procedure when considering their own financial future.

It was against the backdrop of the changing approach of the SRA Rules, the economy, and the developing ambitions of lawyers that, in 2014, we embarked upon the exercise of talking to lawyers around the country to understand their concerns and desires.

We discovered that lawyers were most concerned about:

- No succession or business plans being in place;
- The continuous failure of merger talks;
- Fee earners generating more income than partners;

- The constant pressure to bill, collect monies, introduce new clients, and create WIP;
- The increasing demands of the practice resulting in a lack of work/life balance;
- The rapid exit of fee earners which suggested that pressure was being exerted by the firm's bankers, or there was lack of work;
- Fee earners feeling that they had no value save for billing fees; and
- The inability to retain key clients and generate new clients.

Succession

All of the above factors are variations on a theme and connected to the underlying principle of *succession planning*. In simple terms, if a legal practice is not a successful, attractive business to invest in, then perpetuity of the law firm becomes a question mark and the environment required for succession evaporates.

Lawyers, on the one hand, are asked to bill as much as possible, chase debts, and introduce clients to keep the practice afloat, while on the other they observe a background of failed merger talks and see that there are no plans in place to reward their efforts and provide a stable financial future.

We discovered that lack of planning, and specifically succession planning, was the single greatest concern within the legal sector, not only among lawyers themselves, but also among banks and insurers.

In the majority of legal practices, forward and succession planning simply has not been addressed – often because senior lawyers don't know where to start, or they have no idea how or where to find a solution, or because they are frightened to confront and address the issues facing them, preferring instead to sweep them under the carpet.

Succession and future planning is probably the single most important factor that a law firm should address, yet in law firms up and down the country it is simply being ignored (and indeed this situation is not unique to the UK). When we began to examine in detail other 'new models' on the market, we found that certain issues were being addressed e.g.:

1. Successful, profitable individual fee earners could operate as consultants in a specially created law firm – and be substantially rewarded for the fee income that they generated; and
2. Firms could adopt a common branding, and have the benefit of work being introduced to them – and avoid addressing the restructuring of their current practice.

However, the issues that we felt were not being addressed by existing models included:

- Succession;
- Difficulties around internal politics;
- The failure of the firm to have any direction;
- Financial instability;
- Poor morale; and
- The inability to make the firm attractive to new clients.

By way of example, one of the partners that we met shared his experience of the consequences of failing to provide for succession following a recent merger:

CASE STUDY

Prior to the merger, Firm A had three lawyers each of whom had been with the practice for over 10 years and their total billings were circa. £500,000. When they became part of Firm B, the managing partner of Firm B never sat down with them to explain his business plan for the future or made them feel valued and part of a firm which had a future mapped out for them.

They quickly came to the conclusion that while Firm B's managing partner was quite content to benefit from their billings, he saw no value and thus had made no effort to encourage them or make them feel part of a law firm that they would be proud to be part of. As a result, one of them went to visit a recruitment agent, who also enquired as to whether there were any other lawyers who were unhappy with the merger. Following internal discussions, all three lawyers subsequently gave their three months' notice, and their current clients requested that their files follow with the lawyers.

As a direct consequence, Firm B lost a substantial financial asset (the lawyers), as well as a considerable list of clients. The firm then had to pay recruitment fees to search for replacement lawyers and explain the dramatic reduction of fees in the monthly management accounts to their bankers.

The most important asset of merger – Firm A's three lawyers – was lost for lack of planning, good communication, respect, and reward.

We further found that, in addition to failing to provide for succession, internal politics was perhaps the greatest contributing factor to the failure of a law firm to progress. By way of example, one of the partners we met recounted a discussion at a partners' meeting:

CASE STUDY

> He explained how Partner A had confidently declared that he was the highest biller within the practice that year. In response, Partner B pointed out that if Partner A deducted the costs of his three secretaries and took into consideration his unpaid bills, his billing was not, after all, highly impressive. In fact, he pointed out to Partner A, that if the cost of his three secretaries were deducted and the 80 per cent of the cost of the accounts department that his work demanded were taken into account Partner A had actually made no money for the firm.

This particular high-billing partner with no secretary and minimal unpaid bills was extremely brave; most partners in his position would not voice their opinion for fear of upsetting the partnership relationship. Hence resentments are hidden and issues go unaddressed, with many partners desperate to find their way out of an unrewarding partnership but with no understanding of how this can be achieved.

We also quickly realised that lawyers who can instantly analyse a client's legal issues and recommend solutions, when it comes to their own issues, usually adopt a totally different approach. Legal firms almost always put their clients' interests first – and rarely devote any time to understanding the issues that they must deal with in order to secure their own future.

Creating a different business model

Against the background of so many firms having no succession plans to reassure and maintain their most profitable lawyers, and with many lawyers proving unable to address their own internal political issues, we developed in Lawyers Inc. a new business model. It was designed, not only for individual lawyers but also teams of lawyers and complete law firms, to provide a solution to the most common issues debilitating law firms by:

- Creating a stable legal practice with a focused financial future for every lawyer in the firm;

- Enabling lawyers to progress without having to inject any capital;
- Removing any personal financial liability to the banks and insurance companies;
- Gently persuading our lawyers to obtain monies on account to reduce book debts and assist cash flow;
- Enabling lawyers to increase their client base and development time by transferring all of their practice administration to Lawyers Inc.;
- Adapting to changes in market trends for legal work;
- Utilising the most up-to-date software;
- Operating in the cloud using the latest IT to enable lawyers to achieve a work/life balance, with the opportunity to work from home, or by hot desking, for example;
- Outsourcing services when required to specialised third parties e.g. legal accounts departments and dictation transcription services;
- Reducing expenses by operating a paperless office;
- Reducing expenses while maximising billing, thereby protecting the firm against future changes in government legislation e.g. the increase in court fees and the proposed FCA legislation relating to credit being given in respect of unpaid bills; and
- Introducing systems for cyber security, preserving client confidentiality, and preventing money laundering.

The Lawyers Inc. business model is an ABS designed to emulate the merger or takeover by a successor legal practice. This model completely replaces the traditional succession model for a legal practice and creates a far more attractive relationship between the former junior lawyers and partners.

The model is extremely adaptable and is designed to accommodate any issues that have been stifling the growth and stability of an existing legal practice. All of the lawyers can work together as a 'Pod' at their existing offices if they choose and provide services to their original clients alongside new clients.

The established practice name, which has its own standing and reputation, can be maintained as part of the new group name, if required. None of the lawyers have any liability for indemnity insurance, secretarial and accounts department fees, or a bank overdraft.

The model recognises that professional time is money for a law practice and works to free up lawyers' time to focus on legal work. In simple terms, the former equity partners while no longer in partnership with each other, will become self-employed consultants sharing gross fees with Lawyers Inc., and receiving 60–80 per cent of all of their billings.

Junior lawyers transfer under the Transfer of Undertakings (Protection of Employment) Regulations 2006 (TUPE) to become employees of Lawyers Inc. while still working with their previous partners.

The key to this new modus operandi is a private internal agreement between the former equity partners and their junior lawyers which enables the former equity partners to plan a timeframe for, and terms of, their retirement (e.g. an annuity provided by a percentage of fee income for a few years after retiring). While clients remain under the aegis of Lawyers Inc., the former junior lawyers can plan their future by benefitting from the income stream of the old firm's previous clients. This creates a transparent relationship, freeing younger lawyers to concentrate on helping their clients and generating fee income. Most importantly, the junior solicitors can now create their own careers with confidence and without injecting capital or being exposed to the traditional liabilities of professional indemnity insurance and bank overdrafts.

On average, the law firms that have joined us have increased their net profit by 48 per cent and now have a profitable, financially well-structured future for all of their lawyers, with stability and direction. In addition, they have freed up time to concentrate on marketing and PR for their new firm and we are able to introduce our specialist PR and marketing team who have a proven track record in working with the legal profession. They understand how to attract clients to increase a firm's database and how to promote the ability and skills of each individual lawyer. Lawyers are encouraged to bring their ideas to the table, as part of the marketing plan.

In addition to restructuring law firms, our model equally provides the same benefits to individual lawyers and teams of lawyers looking to maximise potential income from their client services.

It's good to talk – and we will listen

Lawyers provide a service to the public where clients can talk through their legal issues. However, who can lawyers talk to about their own issues and concerns? The Law Society and SRA do not provide any such service, insurers merely provide financial protection for any legal claims, most banks do not provide advice about how to restructure a law firm, and the majority of accountants just produce the annual accounts.

Law firms have few options to sit down and discuss their concerns for their future. We welcome the opportunity to listen. If lawyers can take the time to examine *all* their options, they will be 50 per cent of the way to planning their future. Once they embark on this path they begin to provide their firm with the same excellence of service they provide to their clients.

We don't just want law firms to survive, we want them to thrive.

Chapter 8: Evolving business models in legal services

By Janvi Patel, executive chairwoman and founder of Halebury

The last 10 years in the legal sector have been fascinating. Remember the legal market in 2006? In 2006, I was an in-house lawyer at a global telecoms company. If I needed extra assistance or support I had three options: recruiting additional permanent support; instructing private practice; or hiring a locum – and at that time, the locum market was not very well developed. Those were the options, whether I required assistance for due diligence, contract review, or for assistance on a global transaction. A decade on, we now have a variety of options and this has had a significant impact, not just on the legal profession but also on the business models in legal services.

In this chapter, I am going to discuss how the legal services model has evolved over the last 10 years, the current state of the evolution process, and also what is the next stage.

Traditional law firms

The pyramid model (see Figure 1), as predominately used by traditional law firms, has been in operation for over two centuries. For a large proportion of law firms operating this model, they tend to operate on a '1/3, 1/3, 1/3' model. This means fees earned, and therefore the hourly rate, represents 1/3 towards the fee earners salary, 1/3 towards the firm's operating costs, and 1/3 towards the partnership pot. Of course, there are variations on the model, but generally all roads lead to increasing the billable hours charge, and therefore the 1/3, 1/3, 1/3 revenue generated has been core to the traditional operating model.

The issues both client and lawyer have with the traditional law firm model have been well-documented. However, until recently there were limited alternatives, and the alternative models operating approximately 10 years ago struggled with supply as well as quality control issues.

Therefore, with limited options, clients and lawyers accepted the traditional model.

The above is simply a brief summary. I would be doing a disservice to traditional law firms if I did not mention there are many benefits to the model, ranging from first class training programmes to their management of complex, global transactions. I will leave it to others to comment on them.

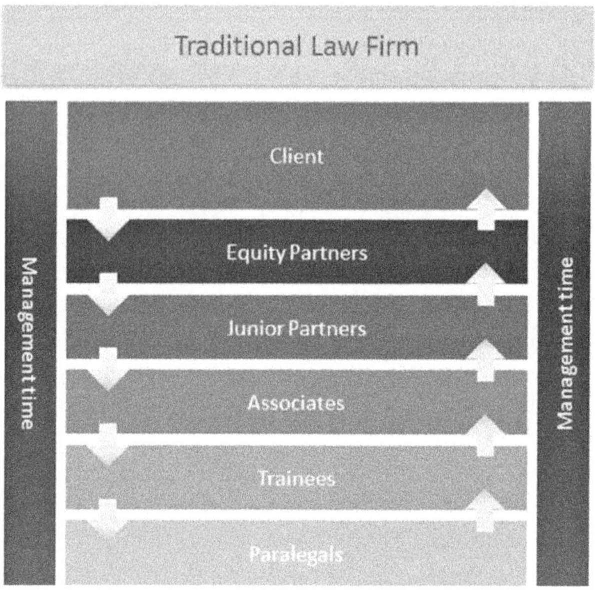

Figure 1: The traditional model

The in-house model

The in-house legal operating model is varied and usually changes depending on a variety of factors; not least, on the size of the team, the budget, the risk appetite of the organisation, and the corporate strategy and vision. Although there may be similarities between various in-house models, I am yet to see the same two operating models, which makes sense as in-house models should be primarily focused on how they support and integrate with their client, i.e. their commercial teams.

However, what is clear is that the size of in-house teams have exploded over the last 10 years and according to the Law Society report 'The Future of Legal Services',[1] this growth is expected to continue. This continued growth has led many GCs and the C-suites to reconsider how their legal teams and spend are managed. In addition to legal tech (which I am also not planning to address in this chapter, and which is addressed elsewhere in this book), there are three key areas that are 'hot topics' within the GC world, all of which are having an impact on the in-house model. I have set these three out below:

1. Motivating and managing an in-house team

As mentioned above, each in-house team tends to have a unique operating model. However, the hierarchy of the in-house legal team is very limited and actually tends to be a flat pyramid structure, which to a large extent mirrors the operating model of traditional law firms, i.e. mid/junior lawyers, associate GCs, heads of legal, in some cases CLOs or COOs, and then the general counsel. Of course, in an in-house team, there is only one general counsel, unlike in traditional law firms where there are many partners.

The flat hierarchy is becoming a growing issue as some in-house teams are larger than some of the largest law firms. How do you manage a team, keep them motivated, help them grow in their own careers, and expand their skill set when there are only a handful of senior positions?

Many GCs have come up with interesting solutions, such as encouraging placements and opportunities within the commercial teams, as well as creating more operational roles to support the legal team, such as CLO or project management roles. Changing the role is an interesting proposition, especially as in-house roles and the skills required are evolving.

2. Cost of external providers

One of the key factors in the growth of in-house teams is the cost of external providers. Remember the 1/3, 1/3, 1/3 ratio? Many GCs feel they can only reduce and control legal spend by cutting 2/3 of that ratio by hiring in. There are of course additional benefits to in-sourcing, such as better service delivery and hands-on advice. However, for many, the key driver is the cost of legal spend.

The cost of external legal spend continues to be an issue and as legal budgets continue to get slashed, many GCs are considering further in-sourcing. A long-term policy of in-sourcing is not a sustainable solution and as a result GCs are looking at more innovative ways to manage their resourcing gaps. It should be noted that in-sourcing will continue to add pressures onto the team structure and exacerbate the point mentioned above regarding motivating and managing an in-house team.

3. Collaborating with external providers

Our legal management consultants from Halebury Consulting partner with in-house teams on how to increase efficiencies, and one of the key areas we consult on is 'how to increase collaboration between external providers and in-house teams'. A significant part of this piece involves looking at increasing collaboration throughout the legal supply chain. At the base this means reviewing the panel review process and better integration between the in-house teams and external providers.

Taking collaboration one step further would involve ensuring that all external providers are collaborating with each other. For example, a traditional law/NewLaw collaboration could mean an in-house team instructs one legal services provider to run a project and that provider has to best allocate the project among the various external providers. In one such case, that could mean a senior lawyer with in-house experience managing the project as part of an in-house team with support from associates from a traditional law firm. Such collaboration is not only cost effective but also incredibly efficient. It is collaboration throughout the entire supply chain.

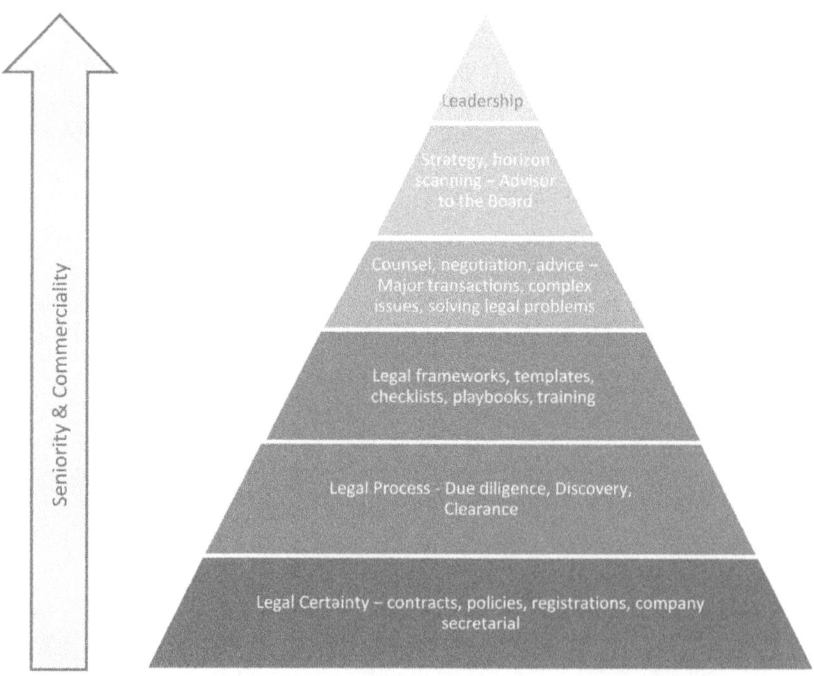

Figure 2: The lawyers within an in-house team

Unbundling legal services

The last 10 years have been fascinating for legal services. Changes such as the introduction of alternative business structures (ABSs), changes in technology, and the drive from GCs for greater change has essentially resulted in the 'unbundling of legal services'.

The unbundling has provided great options for in-house teams. We now have an increase from essentially three options to eight: LPOs, recruitment companies, legal document companies, legal technology companies, e-discovery companies, alternative providers like Halebury, secondary brands such as A&O's Peerpoint or Eversheds Agile, and of course traditional law firms. The market has been blown wide open and, more importantly, within each option there are a number of credible choices.

What is interesting is that the question is no longer, 'I have a piece of work, do I have the capacity to keep it in-house or send it to my traditional law firm, how much will it cost, and where do I get the money to pay for it?' As mentioned above, as an in-house lawyer that was my choice and my decision-making process. We have a much more sophisticated thought process, and in-house teams now analyse the piece of work and allocate work according to where it is on the value pyramid.

As in-house teams are analysing how they operate, a good starting point is the different levels of operation. The pyramid in Figure 2 separates the different levels of the in-house legal team.

Now legal teams look at a number of factors when they are dealing with a piece of work, such as those mentioned in Figure 3.

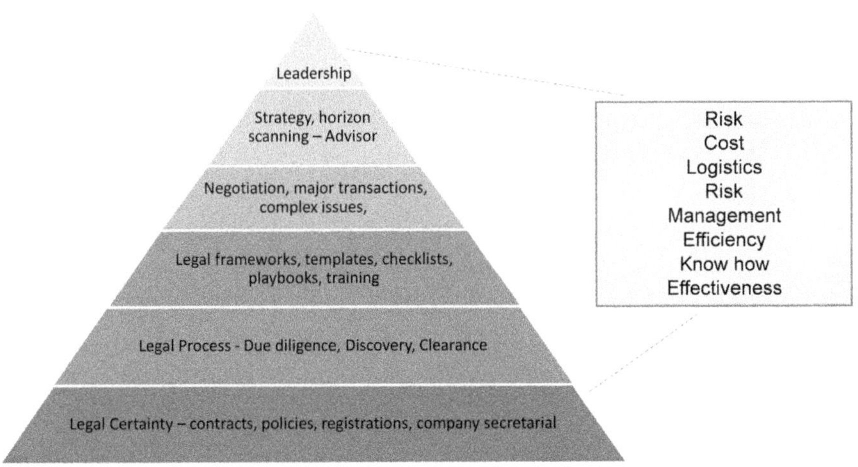

Figure 3: Factors legal teams consider when allocating work

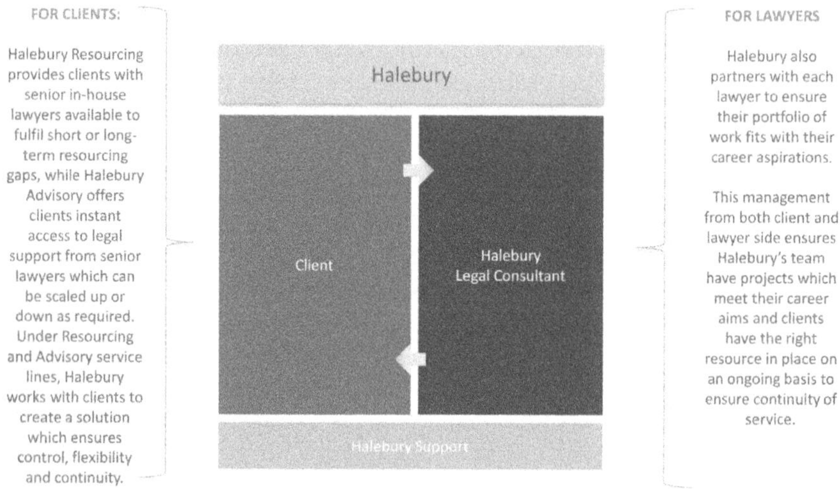

Figure 4: Creating the streamlined Halebury Model

The unbundling has broken down the legal service delivery model to make it more cost effective, more efficient, and more transparent. In-house teams now have a clearer idea of who should do what, and for how much.

Our evolution – The Halebury model

As the in-house model evolves, so does the service provider's model. We created the Halebury model (see Figure 4) in 2007 and we were one of the first to operate in the alternative legal services market, also known as the NewLaw space. The Halebury journey started with asking three fundamental questions: '*why, how, and what?*'.

- **Why** are in-house teams growing so rapidly and why does the profession have an issue with retention, especially at the senior end of the market?
- **How** can we address the issues of both clients and lawyers? Essentially, clients and lawyers need each other and want to work more closely with each other, how can we make that happen?
- **What** does 'good' look like to both parties? If both parties want to work together, maybe the structure and infrastructure in the middle is creating the frustration between the two parties?

We started with a blank sheet of paper and mapped it out from both sides; how could we improve the service delivery for clients? And how could we support our legal team to enable them to achieve their career goals? After analysis and several mind-maps later, we decided that our model would be simple: a team of senior, experienced in-house lawyers who can hit the ground running and slot seamlessly into a commercial team. From our legal team's perspective they would have long-term and direct relationships with the commercial and legal teams as well as a variety of work in a variety of sectors, and to top it all, flexibility. In practice, each lawyer would have four or five clients they would work with on a rotation/flexible basis. The team could then slot into the in-house teams as and when they were needed. The clients could scale up or down on need, lawyers could take time off or have downtime in between projects, and both parties would have knowledge retention and consistency.

The streamlined structure would provide a cost-effective, flexible, and efficient solution for clients and lawyers, which would empower both parties. It was and is a 'win win'.

The model is simple. It provides flexible senior in-house support to in-house teams. We are not the full structure and this is where the unbundling is interesting. In-house teams do not need a one-stop shop. They need commercial, hands-on lawyers who can work as part of their internal team, in line with their internal systems and risk management. It is one of the options available to in-house teams. Figure 5 details where we fit into an in-house team.

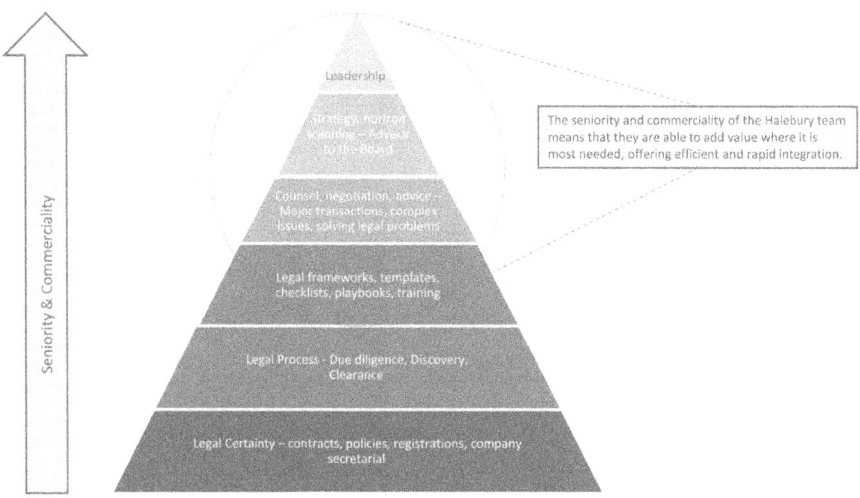

Figure 5: Where Halebury fits into the layers of an in-house team

Next stage of the evolution

There has been a lot in the legal press about the impact of alternative legal service providers and the growth of in-house teams on the traditional law model. One of the most interesting research pieces I have seen is Deloitte's 2016 global research study – the 'Future Trends for Legal Services'.[2] That study states that over half of those surveyed (52 per cent) are considering buying legal services from non-traditional law firms. Another is a research piece by Thomson Reuters Legal Executive Institute in partnership with the Georgetown University Law Center for the Study of the Legal Profession and the University of Oxford Said Business School. This research valued the alternative legal service providers market at $8.4 billion, with the market for contract lawyers, in-sourcing, and staffing services alone valued at $900 million.

Although the alternative legal market is already having an impact on the traditional law firm model and profitability, longer term the growth of the alternative legal market will make a significant dent on the traditional law firm and this will naturally lead to fundamental changes to the traditional law firm model. Indeed, many law firms are already starting to evaluate their operating model going forward. The model illustrated in Figure 6 is already being discussed by a few traditional law firms.

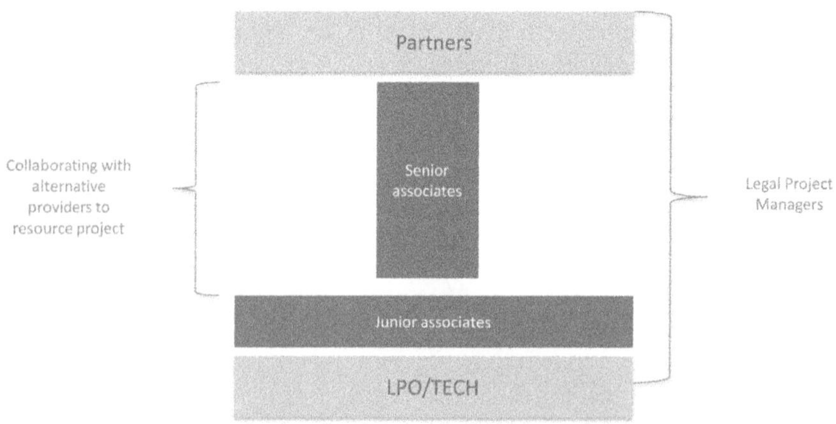

Figure 6: Potential new traditional law model

This new model would require collaboration with external legal service providers and most likely in the alternative service providers space. This is genuine collaboration throughout the legal supply chain. I firmly believe that such collaboration is the future of the delivery model.

It will create more sustainability and efficiency but will also maximise the skills and capabilities within the profession.

Conclusion

A decade ago many in the legal profession talked about 'the need for change', but few imagined the real and fundamental change that has taken place. It is, however, essential that the profession continues to evolve and at every level, from technology, service delivery, to skills training. This journey cannot stop.

References

1. Deloitte, 'Future Trends for Legal Services: Global research study', June 2016. Available at: https://www2.deloitte.com/ro/en/footerlinks1/cookies.html.
2. The Law Society of England and Wales, 'The Future of Legal Services', January 2016. Available at: http://www.lawsociety.org.uk/news/stories/future-of-legal-services/.

Chapter 9: Law firm-client collaboration through the managed legal network

By Richard Tapp, company secretary and director of legal services, Carillion plc and Fleur Kitchingman, senior vice president of legal and corporate secretary, Carillion Canada

Introduction

Carillion is a leading integrated support services company with a substantial portfolio of public-private partnership projects, extensive construction capabilities, and a sector-leading ability to deliver sustainable solutions. The group had annual revenue in 2015 of some £4.6 billion, employs around 46,000 people, and operates across the UK, in the Middle East, and Canada.

With that breadth of activity comes a real need for an integrated, focused legal resource across a range of disciplines. The business works in challenging and competitive markets and must respond both to the bespoke needs of clients and the increasing levels of regulation. Many of its contractual relationships are high-value, individually tailored arrangements demanding significant levels of legal input in structure and design, while its business continues to develop in new markets and new sectors.

For more than a decade, Carillion has built its legal resourcing around a collaborative model using a managed legal network at its heart. The three elements of the model are:

- The in-house team, which focuses on the core areas to the business, principally outsourcing, construction, and project finance;
- A small network of law firms providing targeted advice in other specialist areas, and additional resource in the core areas; and
- Carillion Advice Services (CAS), Carillion's own managed legal service business, which acts as an alternative legal provider for Carillion, our network law firms, and a range of external clients.

The model has worked very successfully in Carillon's UK business, giving access to a range of core support and added value issues. More recently, with the growth of the group's Middle East and Canadian businesses, it has been used to develop relationships in those areas, and this chapter examines the recent successful implementation of managed legal network arrangements in Carillion Canada.

Agenda for change

Carillion's business in Canada has undergone significant change and growth in recent years, developing in new markets and business sectors across the country. At the same time, the business needs were very different to before, and entry into new sectors and provinces demanded a legal resource which allowed us both to serve our existing needs and to be ahead of the game as we changed and evolved and developed our strategy for the future.

We had worked very well with our existing law firms, but at the same time wanted to ensure that they understood how our business was developing, and we also wanted to identify who else we should be working with so that we could continue to align our goals with those of our existing and future business.

Above all, we wanted to follow the model which had served us so successfully across Carillion's businesses worldwide in selecting a limited number of external firms and other legal providers with whom we could form trusted business partner relationships.

We had a clear need for consistency across the business – we are insistent that Carillion Legal has the responsibility for legal resourcing across the business. It is imperative that the same standard and quality of service is delivered across the piece, whether we deliver the work internally, through one or more of our law firms, or through Carillion Advice Services.

As such, collaboration between firms is vital to achieve consistency of service and value – and underlying that, to ensure that there is a real understanding of our business to help us to be proactive around legal issues which affect us now and which will affect us in the future. This in the context of a business undergoing very rapid change and growth, where recently acquired businesses are themselves learning to work together and collaborate to mutual advantage, and where our advisers cannot simply play in one space, but need to understand and embrace the overall picture.

Our aspirations

Using the knowhow and experience from the development of our legal operations and network arrangements in the UK and the Middle East and North Africa (MENA), we wanted to create the first formal network for Carillion Canada. In doing so, we wanted to achieve a spirit of collaboration between our own business, Carillion Legal, CAS, and our chosen providers – not just from a sense of business necessity, but from a desire to achieve real value for everyone involved through understanding, inspiration, and vision of what could be built together. We also wanted to capture the sense of innovation which we had achieved in our legal sourcing elsewhere, not just to deliver better and more cost-effective legal solutions, but to support and develop our business operations across Canada – using the law to enhance the way we do business.

Our processes

The request for proposals

As with most panel selection processes, we ran a process beginning with a request for proposals. We started by pre-selecting a range of firms we thought could contribute both technically, commercially, culturally, and in terms of collaborating with us. We wanted to send a message that we were changing in Canada, and that our approach to external legal providers was also changing.

We stressed the obvious in some ways – even in calling our grouping of law firms a 'network' rather than a 'panel' we wanted to convey the imperative that firms should work together, collaboratively between themselves, rather than seeing us as the only route for communication, discussion, and innovation. We appreciated that this might be uncomfortable for some of firms; our aim was very definitely not to unsettle people, but to inspire people to think differently about the way that legal services were provided.

At the same time, while we were certainly not seeking to buy our legal services by online auction, we did ask all the firms to submit their responses to the request through a single online portal designed purely for tendering legal services. We found this really beneficial in that it allowed us to ensure that all the tendering firms had commonality of information about us, and also to give a completely level playing field to allow us to make a genuine and accurate comparison of the meat of the responses, without being coloured by presentation or marketing.

Communicating the vision

If the request process was helpful to us as a leveller, the in-person presentations which followed it were helpful to give insight into the differences between firms – and between their understandings of our needs. All the firms presented differently, but it was perhaps true that few focused on innovation and collaboration in the way that we sought, and it was clear that we needed to work harder to ensure that people understood what we wanted in terms of excellence beyond the technical. Mirroring our experience elsewhere, finding technical expertise in law firms was simple; what we wanted were those who could build on and use that expertise to develop and grow our business.

Our business had changed significantly in recent years, and even firms we had used for some years were not necessarily familiar with all of our developments, or with our changing strategy. We had to communicate our vision both for the business, and of what was important to us as a client, to help firms understand what it was that we needed. We spent significant time talking to and providing feedback to the firms following this stage, which was a helpful opportunity to talk to each other about expectations and explore how they could be met. It also allowed us to understand better what resources and innovations were available within the firms, developing some real and concrete opportunities which had not been immediately apparent either from prior relationships with firms, or from the formal request process. In particular, we began to understand some of the technical, ICT, and innovation opportunities which were available.

Selecting the network

Self-evidently, we wanted to get the right specialist skill sets, in the right geographies, but also to inject innovation and new thinking. We wanted – and achieved – the introduction of a firm we felt to be particularly strong in this area – and the appointment of that firm helped to act as a catalyst to other firms to share more with us on what they were doing in relation to innovation, and to start to think beyond just the technical expertise. We wanted to keep the network small to allow us to ensure a reasonable flow of work to firms in return for the commitments we sought from them.

Our final selection amounted to seven firms, reflecting the needs and shape of our business: one purely HR-related (Hicks Morley); one purely immigration (Cumming and Partners); three larger national firms (Blake Cassel & Graydon LLP, Norton Rose Fulbright, and McCarthy

Tetrault); one boutique construction litigation firm (Glaholt LLP); and one firm providing broader coverage in British Columbia (Owen Bird Corporation).

Building the team

As mentioned earlier, we see the responsibility for legal advice as that of Carillion Legal – it is not something we can delegate or abrogate to external providers. Conversely, that requires us to build an effective team across the network, and it is important that the relationship partners of each of our network firms must respect each other, be able to work together, be different enough in approach to offer a different perspective without causing tension, and understand that we need them to work together with us and with CAS to achieve a common goal.

In simple terms, the chemistry between us is important, and we do feel we have achieved a relationship where we feel we can learn from each other – both giving, and getting something back in return – using different skills and strengths to do great things. At the same time, though, we have sought to understand that this is a continuing process – we need to proceed at a pace which brings colleagues, internal and external, with us rather than demanding the unachievable and then failing.

Understanding the legal market

One factor in the success of our collaboration is certainly timing – the market in Canada is changing generally with a lot more focus on innovation and technology than before. There is an appetite in the market for change, and for doing things differently, and there is an element of being in the right place at the right time to be able to make the most of that opportunity.

The legal conference

We knew from our previous experience that one tool that was very powerful in bringing people together was a legal conference, to set expectations and to deliver a single level of common understanding of the business, the network members, and the objectives; and also to develop some initial collaborative projects. At the same time, we understood that the concept of a legal conference bringing competing firms together was relatively novel in Canada, and as such we had to communicate in advance, and really well, what the content would be, and the benefits of having the conference. We knew that there were several imperatives:

- **Bringing the right people together** – We invited three or four lawyers from each of our seven firms, together with our business leadership team and some of the key users of legal services, and also our internal lawyers and Carillion Advice Services – about 55 people in total. Where law firms had legal project managers or innovation heads, we invited them too, to add a different dynamic and perspective. We also had an external speaker to highlight the changing marketplace, who also helped to endorse what we were trying to achieve.
- **Providing context** – It was important that we provided clear context, talking to the law firms about the whole of our business, and their place within that business, so that they could see the bigger picture and understand the wider objective. We also talked about how we wanted to provide legal resource as well as what we wanted, with firms collaborating with one another and with Carillion Advice Services – so the overall objective of what we were trying to achieve and the group legal strategy was understood.
- **Building trust** – We appreciated that in order to win the trust of our chosen network firms, we needed also to show the trust was mutual, in terms of sharing the detail of our own business and legal strategies. We needed also to be clear that we understood that the legal conference was a significant investment of time and money on all sides, which reflected the importance of the network to us as a business. It was clear that this helped in terms of the outcomes and need for it to be a success.
- **Showcasing the outcomes of collaboration** – We didn't want the conference just to be a talking shop. The benefits of collaboration need to be seen and felt, and so we used practical workshops focusing on real business issues. We asked for comments in advance to define issues for discussion, which was critical to buy-in to the collaboration exercise. Materials were prepared in advance so participants could come prepared, and feel comfortable with the discussion. We tried to create small, focused, cross-disciplinary groups to solve specific issues, which both focused the law firms on the issue and allowed business colleagues to understand the business, relationship, and cost-saving benefits. The sessions provoked significant and constructive discussion, and were really successful, many attendees citing them as the highlight of the conference.

Collaborating after the conference

A key measure of success of the conference is continued collaboration. As an immediate follow-up, projects have been implemented around environmental compliance, mediation, pre-contract issues, collaboration with CAS, and disputes. We have delivered immediate value through the collaboration of two firms and CAS on a key dispute, and by way of example a series of projects have been initiated in the disputes arena:

- **Improving the delivery of legal advice** – Focusing our use of case assessment tools to ensure we have the best possible understanding of a matter and the commercial imperatives involved.
- **Standardisation of dispute templates** – To develop templates to ensure a common approach to routine litigation matters, consistent with Carillion's preferences.
- **Creation and implementation of knowhow creation, collection, and storage** – To standardise the process to improve knowhow creation, collection, and storage, to ensure a common approach and require effective use of Carillion Legal's online C-Net portal as the repository for commonly used documents.
- **Improvement of the efficiency of the document production process** – Adopting a common suite of guidance, checklists, and precedent documents relating to document review and production in matters large and small, with the objective of controlling costs by providing counsel, Carillion, and CAS with guidance on early engagement with opposing counsel to narrow scope of relevance at the outset, and to leverage technology to produce and exchange relevant documents in a dispute in an efficient and cost-predictable way.

The 'disputes committee' as it has now become known, has gone from strength to strength, and with firms represented by a mix of lawyers, project managers, and knowledge-management and discovery specialists. All participants enjoy the dynamic forum and have worked together seamlessly to present the four different projects, the progress made to date, and their proposed next steps. Most impressive is the interaction between the lawyers and professionals at different firms, who would have little or no opportunity to work together in this way prior to the conference and their participation in the disputes committee.

In all of these areas, we have sought to plant a seed to allow the collaborative creation of ideas, space for them to grow and develop, and to deliver positive and measurable outcomes which have mutual benefit for Carillion, CAS, and the firms involved. We continue to develop relationships through a range of tools, including the C-Net portal, visits to our operations for firms to understand our business better and to build knowhow, and regular relationship meetings which focus not just on reporting but also on innovation and business strategy.

Reflections on collaboration

From our experience with collaborative legal sourcing over many years we know that by creating mutual goals, benefits, and outcomes we have been able to achieve real success through a managed legal network. It has been a pleasure to see that the same tools applied to our growing and developing business in Canada can have the same impact. We are seeing our law firms come together and really enjoy working with each other and with us – not just because we asked them to but much more naturally – and that change has happened in a relatively short timescale.

From an in-house legal perspective, we now do not simply have excellent lawyers advising us in isolation, but we have truly been able to achieve a much higher level of service by bringing all those excellent legal minds together to work as part of a team with our business. It gives speed of response, consistency, quality, and the ability to look ahead at challenges which may arise in the future.

We know that collaboration works. It is a privilege that it allows us to recognise and celebrate the contribution which each member of the team plays in achieving our goals for the network and the broader business.

A version of this chapter first appeared in Slater, L. (ed.) The Bigger Picture: Driving Client Value through Collaboration, *London: ARK Group, 2016.*

Chapter 10:
Business model innovation – Implementing and sustaining change

By Mike Polson, director of Ashurst Advance and co-head of innovation at Ashurst, and Christie Guimond, R&D strategy manager at Ashurst Advance

The traditional law firm business model is facing challenge from a number of drivers, and has been for several years. While claiming that the traditional law firm model is dead or is dying is a popular sport in the legal industry, 'Big Law' has not stood still in the face of these challenges to its business. Many law firms have been transitioning areas of their business to new models which bridge the gap between the law firm model of old and those offered by NewLaw providers.[1] These bridging models will be referred to as 'Evolving Big Law models' in this chapter.

While each law firm has chosen its own evolutionary pathway, and created a variety of new captive and standalone models, the disruption to the traditional business model and ways of working requires an adeptness at delivering effective change. The principles of change management have become an important part of the evolutionary process, and the sense is that only those Big Law firms who can successfully embed organisational and behavioural change will be able to manage the rising challenges to their business.

By focusing on Ashurst's uniquely integrated global service offering, Ashurst Advance, we will explore how we evolved elements of our own traditional business model by creating an Evolving Big Law model, and consider how Big Law can best work to embed these evolved business models in a way which maximises the benefits and sustains change.

Drivers for change

The impact of globalisation, digital technology, increased competition, and de-regulation have culminated in the recent rush by Big Law towards activity linked to innovation and transformation. In addition to these four areas driving the need for change, one of the most significant challenges to the traditional Big Law business model has been the evolution of the law firm/client relationship. Clients' needs and demands have experienced a quantum shift in recent years. In this time, the general counsel role has also evolved to the point where over 88 per cent of GCs are taking a more strategic role in shaping and implementing business strategy, and are being called upon to advise the business on how best to balance commercial opportunities with the risks of decisions that are central to the business' wider success.[2]

Within this context, a widening gap between workloads and budgets has developed, and general counsel and their teams are seeking new ideas and services from their legal service providers to address these pressures by:

- Increasing the efficiency of resources and unbundling legal matters;
- Strengthening the process of managing legal matters through areas such as process improvement, project management, and legal operations; and
- Using technology innovatively by leveraging artificial intelligence, automation, and other emerging digital technologies.

Although a lack of client demand is often cited as an excuse by Big Law not to innovate their business models,[3] clients' needs and demands are now unquestionably the single biggest factor driving change within the legal services market.

Traditional Big Law vs Evolving Big Law models

The Traditional Big Law model

The Traditional Big Law model came into its own in the 20th century, and enjoyed broad adoption by law firms across the globe and general acceptance from clients even into the early part of the 21st century. The model itself is centred around three core components, which are common across most traditional models: 1. organisational structure; 2. revenue model; and 3. value proposition.

Organisational structure

Virtually every sophisticated legal market across the globe adopts the traditional hierarchal 'pyramid' organisational structure, as developed in the early 20th century by Paul Cravath of what is now known as Cravath, Swaine & Moore LLP.

The Cravath system is the foundational structure for the traditional Big Law business model. Until the last decade or so, the system has remained stable and largely unaffected by other forces, with the exception of the development of the two-tiered partnership structure in the 1990s, and a shift in recent years away from exclusive internal promotion towards more lateral hiring. However, the pyramid structure only accounts for the legal organisational structure, and does not cover the many specialist professionals who work across the operational side of the business model.

Revenue model

Linked to its pyramid structure, which relies on full-time lawyers to serve clients, the traditional law firm model is heavily reliant on the billable hours profit and pricing model. The model is predicated on the premise that clients will pay an hourly rate for lawyers' services, which exceeds the law firms' labour and fixed costs, and therefore, as long as the law firm is able to control its cost base and ensure that hours are captured and billed effectively, then the pricing model is a profitable one.

This revenue model has been used by Big Law since the mid-20th century and is deeply embedded in operational processes including financial reporting, annual budgeting, and remuneration.

Value proposition

In traditional Big Law, the value proposition has been focused on an exchange of specialist legal advice between client and law firm. The inherent value of that offering has focused heavily on features such as the capabilities of the law firm, lawyers' credentials, and the history and reputation of the law firm.

The sustained success of the Traditional Big Law model was attributable to an alignment with the *market* for legal services, the *people* working within law firms, and the way legal advice was *delivered*.

The Evolving Big Law model – Changes in alignment

What we have seen in recent years are some significant changes in this alignment:

- **Market** – Increasingly sophisticated purchasers and the growth and development of in-house legal teams;
- **People** – Intensifying war for talent causing significant salary inflation and increased lateral mobility; and
- **Delivery** – An ability to increase leverage driven by a range of factors, including use of technology.

The first part of the 21st century has seen this misalignment increasing. One powerful example is the market demand for global business solutions, of which specialist legal input is just one component, with many clients' needs now crossing traditional disciplinary boundaries.

Looking forward and learning from the evolution of other industries, law is undoubtedly behind broader industry on these key changes to market, people, and delivery.

There is, however, no doubt that we are seeing evolution of the Traditional Big Law model to address this increasing misalignment, with some of the key ingredients of this evolution being:

- **Market** – Using innovation as a key leadership strategy to respond to changing client needs and expectations and ensuring innovation is directly aligned to wider business strategy;
- **People** – Moving beyond traditional core legal competencies into skills areas such as business, technology, project management, and effective collaboration, as well as the ability to work in an increasingly agile way; and
- **Delivery** – Working across geographic, disciplinary, and organisational boundaries.

CASE STUDY

The evolving business model in practice – Ashurst Advance

This need for market alignment was the driver behind our creation of Ashurst Advance. We recognised that there was a need to evolve our own business, in order to bridge the gap between the traditional model and NewLaw models, and we sought to make changes to facilitate this evolution.

Organisational structure

The integrated platform is a captive one, but it does have its own separate leadership structure which has the benefit of facilitating flexible decision-making. We have also adopted a three-dimensional pyramid structure which brings specialist professionals such as legal project managers and legal technologists to the fore of our business and empowers them to work alongside our legal teams.

One of the most significant aspects of our evolution with Ashurst Advance has been to create an integrated business unit which dismantles the traditional 'lawyers' and 'non-lawyers' structural divide which exists within Big Law. Ashurst Advance is a hybrid and recognises the need to respond to market and delivery demands by bringing other professionals alongside lawyers in the frontline delivery of services to clients.

Our expectation is that the scope and scale of influence of other professionals in the delivery model will continue to increase, providing new and challenging career opportunities for those who thrive within an innovative environment.

Value proposition

Ashurst Advance has expanded the traditional Big Law value proposition to other areas of service:

- **Efficient alignment of resource** – We identified that unbundling and efficient use of resource was a critical need for our clients and we developed our Legal Analyst team in Glasgow in 2013. This growing team, which now forms part of Ashurst Advance, has a focus on the recurring work that clients typically seek to unbundle and can provide both legal and operational support.
- **Better application of process to legal work** – Our clients are demanding better value, faster service, and greater cost-certainty and we developed a global legal project management capability within Ashurst Advance to apply rigorous project management techniques to the execution of legal matters across the spectrum of our practices, and to offer specialist project management advice and expertise.
- **Innovative use of technology for service delivery** – Technology is transforming the way our clients do business, and the way legal services are delivered. As part of our Ashurst Advance platform we have created a specialist Legal Technologist team who possess a unique blend of legal knowledge and software development expertise, and can offer enhanced service delivery and technology advice.

Implementing and sustaining change

While it is clear that it needs to evolve, it has often been said that the legal industry is one of the most difficult industries to change because of its business model. Business model evolution has the potential to be transformative for growth and revenue, but it is a highly risky move that can involve a wholesale change to the architecture of a business, and a general aversion to risk is the hallmark of the legal industry. Given that it is widely cited that over 70 per cent of change initiatives fail, a critical challenge for leadership is to understand how to manage the evolution of business models and to ensure that any change is successful and sustainable.

There are numerous models for change management, and Kotter's eight step model (illustrated in Figure 1) is one which is commonly used to provide a framework for those responsible for leading strategic change. The model identifies three key areas of focus, which will each be examined in turn in the context of our experience with Ashurst Advance.

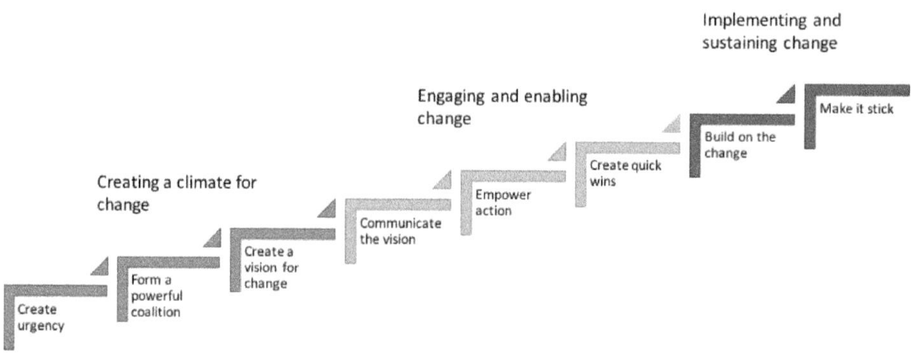

Figure 1 – Kotters' change model[4]

Creating a climate for change

As a first step, it is necessary to create the climate for change by ensuring that there are clear drivers for change and an urgent need, that there is internal support and the right people are in place to deliver the change, and that there is a strong and motivating vision for change.

With Ashurst Advance, we identified the evolving client relationship as one of our key drivers for change. Through in-depth research with our clients, we identified that our clients are facing the dual challenges of rising workloads and squeezed budgets. This potent combination is driving clients to adjust their own ways of working in relation to how they operate and organise themselves, which has a reciprocal effect on their service providers. By recognising that our clients' needs were evolving and that they required more efficient resources, better process management, and innovative use of technology, we were able to identify a vision for our model.

The second challenge we faced was ensuring that we had the right people with the right blend of skills to deliver the change. Choosing the right people to lead the change is essential in inspiring and driving the change across the business.

Engaging and enabling change

People are integral to making change work, but they need to be engaged and enabled. If the need and vision for change is not communicated then the customary response is to resist, and this resistance is a key reason for the failure of many initiatives. The firm's structure, policies, and processes also need to empower action, rather than hinder it and change needs small wins and momentum to generate optimism.

As is often said, the traditional Big Law model by its very nature can hinder change. However, the challenge is not an insurmountable one, as we discovered when we focused heavily on communicating to and engaging with our partner population. For us, it was key to identify champions across our global network who understood the need for change and could help us engage the business by working with us to develop a few key examples of small wins. We also spent time communicating to our legal teams across the globe how the specialist professionals in the three-dimensional pyramid structure could work with them and how such a structure could benefit them at a personal level by allowing them to focus on their own areas of expertise.

Implementing and sustaining change

It is not enough for Big Law to design new business models and to rest on our laurels, assuming that we have done enough to combat the rising challenges. These new models need to be anchored within the law firm's culture, and it is this behavioural change which is the most challenging element of the business model evolution process. One of the key ways to embed change in the long term is to ensure that it is constantly monitored through feedback.

It is this final area of Kotter's model which has been a key focus for Ashurst Advance. In order for our Evolving Business Model to be truly transformative and to meet the needs our clients have identified, Ashurst Advance needs to be embedded in our DNA. We feel that the change process is never over and that we constantly need to be monitoring our progress with our clients and with our legal teams. One of the key ways we do this is by enabling feedback, and by demonstrating active responses to that feedback through tangible examples of improvements we have made or new service areas we have developed.

Parallels with the past?

Although the Big Law Model is described as 'Traditional' it should be remembered that its introduction could actually be categorised as a 'disruptive innovation' at the time! Up until that point, most lawyers were sole traders with only informal office-sharing arrangements and some saw the Big Law model as creating 'law factories' which was not popular. Yet we saw reasonably rapid market acceptance of this as the new 'winning' model.

Those of us engaged in the process of evolving our business models should take confidence from these lessons of the past and be guided by the need to align who we are and what we do to the needs of our markets and our people, and to the way in which legal services need to be delivered.

References

1. Chin, E. "The year Axiom becomes the world's largest legal services firm", 2013, 2018. Available at: http://www.beatoncapital.com/2013/09/2018-year-axiom-becomes-worlds-largest-legal-services-firm/.
2. "Riding the Winds of Change", Ashurst.com, 13 July 2016. Available at: https://www.ashurst.com/en/news-and-insights/insights/thought-leadership-from-ashurst-advance/.
3. "Law Firms in Transition 2017", Altman Weil, 2017. Available at: http://www.altman-weil.com/LFiT2017/.
4. Kotter, J.P., *Leading Change*, Harvard Business Press, 1996.